SURVIVING YOUR PARENTS' DIVORCE

Charles Boeckman

Franklin Watts/New York/London/Toronto/Sydney/1980

Library of Congress Cataloging in Publication Data

Boeckman, Charles, 1920–
    Surviving your parents' divorce.

    Bibliography: p.
    Includes index.
    SUMMARY: Advice for surviving your
parents' divorce. Deals with custody, child
support, visitation rights, guilt, loneliness, re-
marriage, step relatives, and organizations to
turn to for help.
    1. Children of divorced parents—Juvenile
literature. [1. Divorce] I. Title.
HQ777.5.B63   301.42′84   79–24553
ISBN 0–531–02869–0

51995

82-14134

Contents

Acknowledgments

We wish to extend thanks and recognition to the following experts whose help and advice made this book possible:

George A. Constant, M.D., Psychiatrist, Faculty, University of Houston; Director Devereaux Foundation; Private Practice.

Richard E. Davis, M.D., Psychiatrist, Director, Family and Child Psychiatric Clinic, Overland Park, Kansas.

Sharon Duke, Ph.D., Child Psychologist, Corpus Christi, Texas.

William F. Bauman, Ph.D., Child Psychologist, Corpus Christi, Texas.

Loyce Hagens, Ph.D., Professor of Psychology, Corpus Christi State University, and Private Practice.

Richard C. Nelson, Ph.D., Department of Education, Purdue University.

John W. Bloom, Ph.D., Department of Psychology, Northern Arizona University, Flagstaff, Arizona.

Robert Lee Stubblefield, M.D., Child Psychiatrist, Medical Director, The Silver Hill Foundation, New Canaan, Connecticut.

Michael Westergren, Attorney at Law, County Attorney, Nueces County, Texas.

Foreword

This sensitive and psychologically sound book fills a serious void. Most children and adolescents are hurt deeply by the divorce of their parents. Yet excessive pain and permanent damage can often be prevented if parents could offer the child a neutral and authoritative set of guidelines on the expected hazards of divorce. This book is written for exactly that reason. It can be a primer for the child or adolescent, who may be the innocent victim of divorce proceedings. It could also be read by parents considering divorce to enable them to most effectively help their child during the marital dissolution.

Let's face it—these are troubled times for marriage and the family, and any book which can reduce the damaging fallout from broken marriages is an important step in the right direction. Although educational, this book also frequently deals in specifics—in what a child can *do*. It gives concrete suggestions and advice. It names organizations and identifies sources of help for the young person troubled and at sea without guidance. It helps children understand why some parents do fight and why they may be getting a divorce. It helps to explain the legal process involved in the divorce in simple and easy to understand language. It discusses such factors as custody, child support, visitation rights, and so forth. It helps the child understand and gives him or her advice on how to relate to the single parent home after the divorce, how one can best deal with the "holiday blues," and ideas on how to relate more successfully to stepparents, stepbrothers and sisters (if one or both of the parents should remarry).

The book is arranged in clearly identified subsections so that they can be read individually. In essence, this book is emotionally supportive, yet practical. It serves as a sort of "survival kit" for children caught up in the problems of their parents' divorce. Most of all, it helps identify things that a child may *do,* rather than just discussing various problems philosophically.

The few books available on divorce for the young person sometimes come close to hitting the target; but this sound, practical, supportive, and sympathetic book hits the bull's-eye. I heartily recommend it.

Richard E. Davis, M.D.
Director, Family and Child
Psychiatric Clinic, Inc.
Overland Park, Kansas

How This
Book Can Help You

We hear a lot about divorce these days. Statistics show that almost half of all marriages end in divorce. Other couples who don't make it all the way to the divorce courts may fight a lot.

It's good to know that more than half of the couples do stay married, and most people who marry a second time have a happy marriage.

But the fact that you are reading this book shows that you have a personal interest in the subject of divorcing parents. Maybe your parents fight. You're worried that they'll split up. Or they have already told you they're getting a divorce. If that has happened, you are probably feeling confused and maybe frightened. Certainly you are upset—and have every right to be.

It could be your parents are already divorced. You are thinking back over the sad event and trying to get your head together.

After all, having two parents at home is pretty basic to

1

a kid's life. If your parents split up, your future becomes uncertain. You can't see why your parents don't get along, why they have to mess up their lives and yours. You love them both. Why can't they love each other? You might even feel guilty. You might feel somehow responsible. Or you might resent or hate one of your parents, thinking that one is to blame for the problem. Then you may have bad feelings about hating that parent.

There's a good chance you feel a special kind of loneliness, too. Because right now of all times when you could use some reassurance and explanations from your parents, they may be so upset with their own problems they aren't giving you much support.

Or, maybe they tried to talk to you about the situation, but the talk left you unsatisfied. You still have a lot of unanswered questions. Maybe when your parents tried to talk to you they dodged around some personal things. Some things were too painful or embarrassing for them to want to talk about. Perhaps you had things you wanted to ask, but felt awkward about asking. You know, sometimes it's hard for kids and parents to talk about personal things. Some parents give kids a snow job. They're not able to give straight answers. They may treat you like a baby.

Your friends might not be much help, either. You may be too embarrassed to tell them about this trouble at home, afraid they won't like you if they find out your parents are divorcing. And it's a personal matter with you. Besides, your friends probably don't have much helpful information to give you unless they have been through the same situation in their lives. And even if they have, their parents and their problems are not the same as yours. Friends can be wonderful support during troubled times, but they can't help you sort out what is right and what is wrong.

So, you're feeling lonely and confused.

You're going to be coping with a lot of emotions during your parents' divorce—your own emotions as well as the emotions of your parents, and the emotions of your brothers and sisters. In most cases, divorce is an emotional upheaval in all the lives it touches. And even though it is your parents who are divorcing or separating, it is going to have an impact on your life.

There's just no escaping the fact that your life is going to be changed by all this. It may involve drastic changes, like moving to another part of the country with one of your parents and starting a new life. Or the changes could be minor. But there will be changes.

What you need at this point is some useful information about yourself, about your parents, and about the whole complicated matter of divorce. You need to know something about the way you are feeling, and what to do about those feelings that can get to be so overwhelming. It might help to know something about the actual procedure of getting divorced as well as things such as "child custody," "support payments," "visiting rights," how to adjust to stepbrothers and stepsisters, and how to adjust to stepparents. Also, there are a number of organizations and places you can go to for help and advice. You should know how to contact them. They might bail you out of a really tough situation.

Some kids find their parents' divorce so upsetting they want to visit a counselor or psychologist or a psychiatrist for a while to get their lives back on the track. That might be frightening to you. But there is absolutely no reason for you to feel that way.

A lot of kids think only crazy people have to go to a psychologist. Not so. In fact most people who go to psychologists or psychiatrists aren't crazy at all. They go because life has gotten them down. They feel bad because they have a lot of mixed up or sad feelings. They may have problems about their job or marriage, or how they get along with other people. A psychologist or psychiatrist can help them with these problems and usually can make them feel a lot better and happier.

A lot of people don't understand the difference between a psychiatrist and a psychologist. (The slang term for those doctors is "shrink" or "headshrinker.") Both of these kinds of doctors have had many years of training. The difference is that a psychiatrist is also a medical doctor. He can prescribe medicine as well as talk to you. A psychologist is usually called "Doctor," too. But a psychologist does not prescribe medicine. This kind of doctor talks with patients and may give different kinds of tests to better understand the patient's personality and problems.

School counselors and social workers can also help children who feel bad over their parents' divorce. Other places where children can find this kind of help would be through family agencies, mental health clinics, and child guidance clinics.

These counselors, psychiatrists or psychologists can help you find the right answers if life gets you down. They can be sympathetic and understanding friends.

You may think of this book as a kind of handbook for kids whose parents are splitting up. You can pick it up any time and turn quickly to the part that will give you the information you need. It is arranged so the table of contents and chapter subheadings are a guide to what you want to know.

Events in life aren't nearly so frightening and complicated if you know what to expect. It's the unknown and unexpected that scares us all.

HELPING YOU MAKE CHOICES
THAT ARE GOOD FOR YOU

At this point in your life you can make some choices that are important. If you have a good understanding of what your options are, you'll be better off. You can then often make wiser and better-informed choices. Your problems won't go away, but you will feel better and probably have a lot easier time of it in the difficult months ahead.

Most people get through life more successfully and are happier most of the time when they discover they can make choices in their life. They find they don't have to just stumble along the same blind path.

You are able to make smarter choices when you understand what is going on; when you understand why you feel the way you do and behave the way you do. Getting all the information you can is important when you're up against something big in life—and that certainly includes divorcing parents.

What do "choices" have to do with the fact that your parents can't get along with each other and the general mess your life is in? To begin with, your parents made a choice when they picked each other, which, it turns out, may not have been the best choice they ever made. But that was not altogether their fault. No one has yet come up with a sure-fire formula for getting two people together who will live happily ever after, in spite of what the fairy tales say. It's quite possible for adults to fall out of love just as they fell in love. That may happen if their personalities and emotional needs change with the passing years so that one no longer finds the other attractive or appealing. If one marriage partner grows tired of the other in a physical sense—that is, no longer finds the other sexually exciting—he or she may interpret that to mean they are no longer "in love."

Someone once joked, "Marriage makes strange bedfellows." We are all unique individuals, each with his or her complicated set of needs and hang-ups. Sometimes after two people are married a while, they discover their mate isn't at all like they thought he or she was. Sometimes one, or both, change so much over the years that they become strangers to

5

each other. They are so different in their needs and interests that they are, indeed, "strange bedfellows." Their personalities may become like two pieces of sandpaper rubbing against each other.

Fortunately, this doesn't always happen. There are many, many happy marriages. Couples still do fall in love, marry, have a family, and stay in love and are faithful for the rest of their lives.

However, in the case of your battling parents, the age-old fairy tale of falling in love and living happily ever after didn't come true. So they have made another choice, which is to obtain a divorce.

When that happens a whole bunch of new choices that you probably wished you didn't have are going to be facing you.

Before the family trouble started, your choices probably involved such matters as how to make friends, how to study to make passing grades, what clothes to wear, what records to buy, how to spend your allowance, what movies to see. But when you live in a home with parents who aren't getting along with each other, you are faced with much heavier choices.

In situations where battling or divorcing parents are involved, there may not always be simple, clear-cut answers as to which choice is best for you to make. There may be choices about how to deal with the feelings that are tearing you up. You may have to make a choice about what you should say or do when one parent asks you questions about the other parent, or when one parent is saying bad things about the other parent. Sometimes you may be faced with the serious choice of whether you should call the police if an angry or drunk parent is threatening to physically harm the other parent.

Then later, after the divorce, you face choices about your new relationship with your parents (the one you live with most of the time and the one you visit), and perhaps further down the road, your relationships with stepparents, stepbrothers, and stepsisters.

Another thing: not all parents who get divorced battle openly. Your parents might be the kind who hold in the pain and hurt and anger they are feeling. Their friends and relatives may not dream they are having trouble and are shocked when they hear about the divorce. But you sense your parents are not happy with their marriage, even though they don't talk about it openly. In this situation you may have choices to make about handling or dealing with your feelings that would be different from a kid whose parents yell and argue and slam doors.

CHOICE AWARENESS— WHAT IT MEANS TO YOU

"Choice awareness" is a term with a special psychological meaning that is used by Dr. Richard C. Nelson and Dr. John Bloom, who have written several articles and a book on the subject. There are other, similar approaches to taking responsibility for your own life and actions. But we like the term choice awareness. This term focuses your attention on a special way you can be in better control of your life.

What it boils down to is becoming aware that you can stop and make a conscious choice in almost any situation before you act. You don't have to go on reacting in the same old way. Most of us make our choices out of habit. When a situation comes up, we react in our established pattern without even thinking about it. We let our emotions and the habits we have formed over the years make our choices for us. That doesn't give us much control over our lives, our feelings, how we get along with other people, or much control over our future.

If we can hold up for a second or two instead of blindly

jumping into the same old pattern, and if we'll review the options we have, then we might make a smarter and more productive choice.

Let's apply this approach to your situation.

If your parents are fighting and are on the verge of a divorce, you could just do nothing. You could keep all your feelings bottled up inside yourself, growing more depressed and miserable, more withdrawn. *Even deciding to do nothing is making a choice.*

But a better choice might be to talk to someone about your feelings. Just getting your thoughts and feelings into the open, putting them into words, can sometimes make you feel a lot better. It's important, though, to talk to the right person. You might try and talk to someone who either won't listen, or, without meaning to, will make you feel worse than you already feel. One girl tried to tell her aunt about how bad she felt over her parents' getting a divorce, and how at times she felt as if she hated her mother for wanting the divorce. Her aunt didn't want to listen to the girl talk about her private feelings. "It's sinful to hate your parents," she warned.

The aunt was very wrong. Many kids do feel anger and hatred toward one or both of their parents when their parents divorce. The kid can't help it. It's a natural emotional protest against the hurt and sorrow the divorce is causing the child. And it is better for the kid to talk about it, to get it off his or her chest, than to keep it smoldering inside and brood about it. But the aunt's reaction made the girl feel terribly guilty about feelings that she couldn't help.

So try to talk about your feelings to someone who is sympathetic and understanding.

If you can't talk to your parents and you're too embarrassed to talk to your friends about your trouble, you could talk to your minister, to a teacher you like, or to your school counselor. Getting your feelings out in the open may help take off some of the pressure.

8

It's also good for you to know that even though this may be a trying time in your life, most kids survive their parents' divorce pretty well. Studies have shown that after a period of adjustment, children of divorced parents don't necessarily get into any more trouble than other kids. They do okay in school. Some may even be happier when the divorce is over, and they don't have to live in a home where bickering parents keep things in a constant emotional turmoil.

Some famous people have come from homes where their parents were separated or divorced: actors Charles Chaplin, Ethel and Lionel Barrymore, Maurice Chevalier; dancer Nijinsky; architect Frank Lloyd Wright; artist Toulouse-Lautrec; cartoonist Bill Mauldin; jazz musician Louis Armstrong; athlete Jackie Robinson; and composers Sergei Rachmaninoff and Sergei Prokofiev, to name just a few.

You probably will find this hard to believe now, but living through your parents' divorce could be a positive experience in your life—a chance to understand yourself better, to know more about your feelings and the feelings of adults. And that helps you understand others—people your own age, too—which means you make friends easier and in general handle life better.

In the next chapter you will read how "choice awareness" can be a useful, practical tool that you can use in dealing with problems that fighting parents cause in your life.

CHAPTER 2

What To Do
When Your Parents Fight
All The Time

Becky thought desperately, "It's almost five-thirty. Dad will be home any minute now. I have to get out of the house."

The feeling of dread was growing inside her.

She had reached the front door when the phone rang. "Becky," her mother called, "it's Miss Devon."

"Oh, no!" Becky thought with a sinking feeling. "Not now of all times." She hesitated, her hand on the doorknob, wondering if she could just keep on going.

"Becky!" her mother called impatiently.

Becky felt pulled in two directions. She wanted to speak to Miss Devon, the school yearbook sponsor. But not now— not at this bad time. . . .

But she had no choice. She turned back to the hall and picked up the phone with damp, nervous fingers. "Just today, let them not fight," she prayed.

Then she heard the back door slam. Her gaze flew to the hall clock. Five-thirty. Her father was home from work.

10

Becky swallowed hard. She tried to keep her voice normal as she spoke into the phone. "Hello. . . ."

"Hello, Becky," Miss Devon said in her pleasant, soft voice. "I have good news for you."

"You—you do?"

It was starting in the kitchen. Her father's loud, angry voice, "Listen, get off my back will you?"

Her mother's shrill, "What a fool I was to marry a two-timing rat like you! You just can't keep your hands off that little tramp in your office, can you?"

"You're crazy, you know that?" her father yelled. "You're a crazy woman. You ought to be locked up . . . !"

Becky tried to cover the telephone mouthpiece with a trembling hand. Through the pounding in her head she heard Miss Devon telling her that she had been appointed to the yearbook staff. It was the exciting news Becky had been praying for. But now all she could think about was the shameful yelling and cursing between her parents, and her fear that Miss Devon would hear them. Miss Devon was such a kind, soft-spoken, refined lady. Becky was desperately ashamed for her to know what went on between her parents. Maybe if Miss Devon knew about the ugly fighting that went on in Becky's home, she wouldn't want Becky on the yearbook staff.

Lately, the fighting started the minute her father came home from work, at five-thirty. Becky tried to get out of the house before then. She'd go to the library, or over to see her best friend, Linda—anything to get away.

Somehow she made it through the telephone call, worried and embarrassed as the angry shouting between her parents went on. Then she hung up. Her heart was a heavy lump. This should have been a great moment for her. She should have been able to run to her parents with the news that she had been picked as yearbook staff photographer. Instead, she fled to her room. There, she curled up on her bed in a miserable ball and sobbed into her pillow.

You have a lot of problems to deal with if you live in a home where parents are engaged in constant warfare. You may feel as if you're in "no-man's land," dodging stray bullets.

Your school work can suffer. So can your health.

If you have the kind of parents who yell and argue and insult one another, you might feel like crawling in a hole. If the fighting starts at night and goes on past midnight, it can interfere with your sleep.

On the other hand, you might have the kind of parents who give each other the silent treatment. That can be just as bad in a different way. This kind of anger between parents doesn't come out in words or physical blows. It just turns the atmosphere in the home into cold lead. There's a chill in the air. The resentment between your parents makes the atmosphere so heavy sometimes you feel as if you can't breathe.

You know they must not love each other. When one parent comes home, the other doesn't greet him or her. They may have separate bedrooms. They never embrace or show one another any affection. They give one another the "silent treatment." Days may go by without them exchanging a word. A family meal is a silent, strained event.

Actually, most married people have fights from time to time. It would be pretty unusual for two people to be together all the time and not have a falling out now and then, just as you do with your friends. And there are deep emotions involved in marriage that can explode. Kids don't always understand this, but sometimes it's healthy for Mom and Dad to have a squabble. They get things off their chests that way. They express their feelings openly, clear the air, and afterward feel better about each other.

If your parents have an occasional battle, but resolve their difficulties, kiss and make up and show affection for one another between fights, then it's nothing for you to get upset over. Just keep out of their way until the storm blows over. Be glad they have strong feelings for each other.

12

But when there is chronic fighting that gets progressively worse, or if there is a sudden, terrific blowup over a serious matter such as one parent discovering the other parent had sex with a third person, then they may have a problem with their marriage that is so bad it can't be resolved. It's possible they will separate or divorce. You need to be realistic about that. The divorce could be a relief and it clarifies the situation for the children.

One parent may say to you, "Our divorce is an act of love for ourselves and our children. We are divorcing to restore some peace and sanity to our individual lives because our life together is a disaster."

Some parents, even though they hate each other, go on living together "for the sake of the children." It's tough on the kids either way. Either they must live in a home where there is constant bickering or animosity, or they must adjust to their parents being divorced.

Melissa, a young teenager, told her counselor, "I hate it at home with them fighting like that all the time. I just want to pack up and run away."

A CHOICE THAT WILL HELP YOU— SELF-CONCERN (ONE OF THE MOST IMPORTANT CHOICES WE CAN MAKE)

If your parents are constantly fighting and making your home life miserable, you may have to stop worrying so much about your parents and think about yourself. You might call it "self-concern." You need to become concerned about your own life and what is best for you since you are not going to be able to fix the problems between your parents, as much as you wish you could. That's something only they can do.

This self-concern business is a difficult and a grown-up choice for a kid to make. You have been conditioned to think of your life revolving around your home and family. That's

13

where you are expected to get a great deal of your emotional support and love through your adolescent years. But until your parents resolve their differences one way or another they won't be able to give you a normal, happy home life. They are too involved with their own emotional troubles. So you may have to take charge of your own life. You can do that by filling your time with activities and interests that keep you busy in a wholesome way and allow you to spend less time at home.

There is much to gain in this move toward independence if you carry it out in a positive way. It's a big step toward becoming an adult. And it's good to find out you can rely on your own self.

Relatives can be a big help. If you have an aunt or uncle or cousin you like, or grandparents nearby, you might see if you can spend more time with them until things are better at home.

Friends are important to someone your age. Probably you have a best friend. Spending time with your best friend and your best friend's family can fill some of the gaps in your own family life.

Perhaps you have an older brother or sister living away from home. They understand the problem you're having and might welcome your spending more time with them. You need to be sure, however, that your relatives welcome the extra time you want to spend with them, and that you're not making a pest of yourself.

There are many activities at school and after school that can add new dimension to your life. If you are in middle school or junior high, you might become involved in the band or choir. If you have a lot of school spirit, you could go out for cheerleading or twirling. If you are the athletic type, sports can become important in your life.

When you're in high school, there are more extracurricular options open to you: such as the drama club, foreign language clubs, chess club, and other groups. You could work on the yearbook staff or school newspaper, join an academic club or be on the school council. In high school, band and choir members often get to take some out-of-town trips.

Many young teens find it's great to start earning their own money. You are never too young to begin a business career. And you'll have extra spending money in your pocket. There are jobs you can do like baby-sitting, yard work, newspaper delivery routes and car-washing. Some communities have "Hire-a-Teen" projects in the summers that can help you land temporary jobs during vacation. Your local newspaper or city hall can tell you about things like that. Or, run your own ad: "Teenager for hire. Any odd jobs appreciated." Being paid for something you do gives you the independence to buy things for yourself or save for college, and it makes you feel good about yourself.

One enterprising youngster in Texas began selling CB radios out of his parents' garage when he was in high school. By the time he graduated, he owned his own store and was a successful young businessman.

Another thing that can make you feel good and can offer an escape from an unhappy home situation is doing volunteer work at a local hospital or nursing home.

You might also give some thought to your talents and hobbies.

If you like to act, many towns have community theaters that put on special productions for young teens or welcome your help backstage, working on sets. You might want to take music lessons, dance lessons, art lessons, or go to sewing classes. A lot of kids these days are becoming involved with photography. Your school might even have classes in picture taking and darkroom procedure. If not, check with your local college or university about night classes in photography, or just go to your public library and read up on the subject.

Collecting things can be fascinating. One girl began picking up shells on the beach. Soon, she was reading up on the names of the shells she found and classifying them. Her collection of shells grew. When she became an adult, she wrote a book about shells.

You can collect almost anything that interests you: stamps, coins, Indian arrowheads, old bottles, antiques, old books and magazines. Some of these collections may become quite valuable.

The Boy Scouts, Girl Scouts, Campfire Girls, and 4-H clubs are organizations that can help you make friends and fill your time with interesting activities, camping trips, and various projects.

Many young people find great comfort in strong religious beliefs. In their faith, they find a love that takes the place of the love they're missing at home. Your church can be one of your best emotional supports, especially if it has a good youth program. It may have opportunities for you in the choir, in youth groups, summer camps, retreats, and other social functions, along with regular church and Sunday school. You might enjoy teaching a Sunday school class for younger children or helping out in the nursery.

Being realistic about it, none of the things we've mentioned are going to completely take the place of a happy home life and parents who get along well together. But these things can make it easier for you if you don't have a happy home life. They can keep you busy and make your life interesting and fun, so that you don't spend all your time dwelling on your parents' problems, worrying about what's going to happen, withdrawing into yourself and becoming more lonely and depressed.

It's what some people call making the best of a bad situation.

The important thing is to become aware that you can make choices in your life. You don't have to just drift along in the old, habitual pattern, pushed this way and that by circumstances, feeling sorry for yourself and making things worse for you and your parents.

Learning consciously to think about making choices gives you a better grip on your life.

Next, we'll talk about the feelings you have, and what to do about them.

CHAPTER 3

What To Do About Your Own Feelings

"All right, kids, let's get those instruments out."

Mr. Clements, the school band director, bustled about, getting the band ready to march.

Sarah opened her clarinet case. It was a hot day, here in the Mexican border town. People around her were laughing and talking. Some of the kids were blowing their horns, rattling the snare drums. The midday sun shone brightly on the Mexican plaza with its bright red and blue tiled benches.

The other kids were perspiring in their green band uniforms. But Sarah felt strangely cold. She hadn't been feeling well all morning. Now the feeling was growing worse. Her stomach was churning. She felt light-headed. There was a sensation of unreality about things going on around her. And she couldn't seem to get her breath.

She sat on one of the tile benches and tried to put her clarinet together. But her fingers were shaking so badly she couldn't get the instrument assembled. She tried to fight down the bad feelings. She thought, "I can't get sick."

Everyone else was having a great time. The trip down here on the school bus had been exciting. For weeks, the band had been rehearsing for this border town parade. It should have been a carefree day for Sarah. But it wasn't. She was feeling worse by the minute.

Now she couldn't hold back the tears.

Within a few moments Mr. Clements was at her side. "Sarah, what's wrong?"

"I—I don't know," she whispered. Her teeth were chattering. "I—feel sick. . . ."

The band director motioned to a band sponsor, Mrs. Snyder.

Sarah felt confused. The next thing she knew, she was back in the school bus. Mrs. Snyder, a kind, motherly woman, was hovering over her. Sarah heard the band play as they marched off.

"You're going to be all right, Sarah," Mrs. Snyder comforted her. "I'm taking you to the airport in my car. We'll have you home in a couple of hours."

"I—I don't know what's wrong," Sarah whimpered. "I feel so scared. . . ."

Mrs. Snyder kept talking to Sarah. She talked steadily in a low, soothing voice. Sarah hung onto the sound of Mrs. Snyder's voice. She felt as if she were drowning and only the band sponsor's voice kept her from sinking forever.

On the way to the airport, Sarah suddenly blurted out, "Is this what it's like to have a nervous breakdown?"

Mrs. Snyder gave her a thoughtful look. "I don't know, dear. Is that what you think is wrong?"

Sarah wasn't able to reply.

She heard Mrs. Snyder ask if something was bothering her. She couldn't answer that, either. It was too hard to talk about. It was all locked up inside her, along with the bad, frightening feelings that had been churning around inside her ever since she found out her parents were getting a divorce.

ONE OF THE WORST FEELINGS YOU MAY HAVE

Psychologists call it "separation anxiety" or "separation fear." This is the kind of bad feeling that lurks in the deep recesses of our mind. It may go back to earliest childhood: the fear of the baby that it will be lost from its mother. It's a sad, frightening, demoralizing feeling we have about being separated from the security of loved ones and safe surroundings.

Put another way, you could say that a child is afraid his or her parents will go away. Dr. Graham B. Blaine, Jr., a psychiatrist, wrote about it this way, "One of the most powerful unconscious fears of a child is that he or she will be deserted and abandoned by one or both parents."

This is a fear that is hard to deal with. It is hard to reason with a fear like this. It's like a phobia. The bad feeling comes over you in a dark, frightening wave. You are demoralized. All you can think of is that the divorce means one of your parents, whom you love, is going away. He or she will be lost to you forever.

Indeed, some experts have described divorce as being like a death in the family.

But this isn't the case at all. Your parents are not divorcing you. They are divorcing each other. They may have stopped loving each other. They haven't stopped loving you. And even though one of them may not be living under the same roof with you after the divorce, you will probably still see them both.

Of course, there are cases where a parent just deserts his or her family. To be realistic, there are parents who simply don't love their kids. But in the vast majority of cases, even

20

though divorced, parents will continue to take care of their children and love them.

Probably, you will live with one parent and visit the other. You may even see more of your parents after the divorce. The parent you visit may give you more attention than when he or she lived at home.

Whatever the outcome of the divorce, there is going to be someone around to love you and take care of you.

One way you can deal with this fear on an emotional level is to bring it out in the open and talk about it with your parents. Some kids are ashamed to talk about feelings like this. It's nothing to be ashamed about. Tell your parents frankly how you feel. "I'm afraid after the divorce you'll go away and I'll never see you again. You won't love me any more."

In most cases, parents will reassure a kid in a way that will help a lot to relieve this bad feeling.

WHAT TO DO WHEN YOU ARE ANGRY

"Hey! Fight!"

A small crowd quickly gathered on the school grounds. A tall, skinny boy, his freckles bright on his pale angry face, was facing another boy who outweighed him by twenty pounds. "I'm going to break your face, Willie!" cried the thin boy and swung wildly.

Then the school principal descended on the crowd and broke up the fight. "Down to the office, you two. Mark, you're in big trouble! This is the second fight you've been in this week!"

His real name was Mark, but the kids all called him "Stringbean." At fourteen, he was nearly six feet tall. He looked as if he didn't weigh much more than a pair of tennis shoes. "All eyeballs and kneecaps," his uncle teased.

Mark didn't mind being called Stringbean. Being tall gave him a certain status in his school crowd. He was good-natured. His freckled face was often split by a wide grin. And he discovered that his gangling height gave him a big edge on the basketball court.

"Stringbean, you're going to wind up a basketball pro," his coach encouraged him.

Then Stringbean's personality began to change. He became withdrawn and sullen. His friends couldn't understand what was eating him. He became touchy and belligerent. The old, fun-loving Stringbean vanished. Now he had a chip on his shoulder.

The afternoon after Stringbean's fight on the school grounds, his basketball coach talked to him in the locker room. "Mark, what's eating at you? We're on the way to having a district winning team this year. But you're messing the whole team up. You make fouls, start fights. You act like you're mad at the world. The principal is talking about expelling you."

Stringbean sat on the edge of a locker-room bench, his head bowed. Suddenly, large tears filled his eyes.

If it had been anyone but the coach talking to him this way, Stringbean would have just become more sullen. But there was a special bond between him and his coach. His coach was like a second dad. He knew the coach wasn't just chewing him out, the way the other teachers did. His coach really cared.

Suddenly, the dam broke and Stringbean began pouring out all the misery that had been eating at him for weeks. Between tears, he told his coach about the trouble he was having at home. His parents were going to get a divorce.

Stringbean was bewildered and angry at what was happening. He was angry with his parents for letting things get in such a mess, for robbing him of a happy, normal home. At times he felt as if he hated his parents. He wanted to yell at them and hit them for doing this to him. But he couldn't do

22

that. He kept all the anger bottled up inside. He couldn't talk to his parents about how he felt. They were off in another world, their own world, wrapped up in their own problems. They hardly seemed to know he existed these days. And he was ashamed to talk to anyone else about the situation.

The anger inside Mark had to come out somehow, so he got into fights, picking on other kids in school and being belligerent on the basketball court.

That's the tricky thing about angry feelings. They won't just dissolve. They can come out in disguised ways. If you are angry at one person about something, but don't tell him or her, you may take it out on someone who has nothing to do with the reason you're angry.

It's like the boss who left home in a bad mood because his car wouldn't start. When he got to the office, he chewed out his secretary about something trivial. He was really mad at his car, but since he couldn't kick his car, he substituted his secretary.

You may get sore at a friend because he lost your notebook. You don't jump on him about that because you know he didn't do it deliberately. Still, you're irritated at him, and later that day, you might pick on him about other things. He can't figure out why you're so grumpy at him, and neither can you. Actually, you're still bugged about the notebook incident, though you think you've put it out of your mind.

Sometimes when people are angry they take it out in the way they drive. They're hostile behind the wheel, honking impatiently, yelling at other drivers, and zooming through traffic in a belligerent way. That's a dangerous thing to do with one's angry feelings. It causes lots of wrecks.

Other people take it out on themselves. Kathy had chronic headaches. She'd had her eyes tested, but new glasses didn't help. And her stomach was upset all the time. She'd lost a lot of weight the past year. Sometimes, if she had a pizza with her friends, she'd throw up. Other times, her stomach woke her, hurting at night. Her doctor found she had an ulcer.

Kathy's parents were getting a divorce, and she had a lot of bitter, angry feelings about it. She felt her parents had let her down. In Kathy's eyes, they were being selfish. But Kathy swallowed her feelings. Most of the time, she tried not to think about it. But anger is a powerful force. It can wreck things inside as well as outside. In Kathy's case, since it did not attack something on the outside, it attacked inwardly, causing psychosomatic illness. Her smothered anger made Kathy physically sick.

Bottled-up anger can make you feel badly depressed. You may not realize how angry you are. You keep angry feelings submerged or repressed because you think it isn't right to hate your parents. Sometimes the anger is so well hidden from yourself you have to talk with a therapist or counselor to uncover the feelings. Then you may be surprised to discover how deep and furious your hidden anger had been.

Angry thoughts won't injure other people. It's normal, at times, to feel angry with people we love a great deal, even hate them. It is healthier for you to realize that you do feel angry, than to be ashamed or afraid to let those feelings enter your mind.

What can you do about your angry feelings? It may help if you can talk to your parents directly about how the situation at home is making you feel. If you explain how their fights are making you feel sick inside, how they are disrupting your school work and generally making you miserable, and how angry you feel about it, it is possible your parents might be jolted into going to a marriage counselor to iron out their problems.

You need to talk about your anger as calmly and objectively as possible with your parents without actually losing your temper and yelling. Expressing your anger in a constructive way means you talk about how you feel inside. You might say, "I'm so angry I'd like to clobber somebody." You don't actually pick up a club and do it. No doubt that would relieve your tension, but it would also relieve the other person of his or her scalp and relieve you of your freedom when they put you in jail. In a civilized society, verbalizing your anger constructively means explaining how you feel inside—talking it out—without actually acting out your primitive, destructive feelings.

If you can't talk to your parents, it will help to talk out your angry feelings with somebody who will listen and understand. That person might be your school counselor, teacher, coach, friend, relative, or minister. In Stringbean's case, he was able to talk out his anger with his coach. It was like a safety valve, letting off his steam. It helped him through the rough time of his parents' divorce, and he was able to keep his place on the team.

It may also help you to sit down and write out your feelings in a letter or diary. You might keep a daily journal, writing in it all your personal thoughts and feelings. You could consider your journal a friend in whom you can confide—someone you can tell all your deepest feelings.

Sports can be a healthy way to overcome the destructive forces of angry feelings. And sports can help fight depression. Smashing a tennis ball, knocking down bowling pins, hitting a baseball, tackling a football opponent, running until you are tired—these are wholesome, socially-acceptable outlets for aggressive feelings.

WHEN YOU ARE DEPRESSED

Many kids, when their parents are going through a divorce, have so many sad, angry and mixed-up feelings that they become depressed. When you are depressed, you don't feel like talking with people, and you don't want to make friends. You may lose your appetite. You have trouble going to sleep, or you may want to sleep all the time. You can't concentrate. You don't feel like doing anything. All your systems kind of shut down.

You have no energy or interest and have to force yourself to become active in your daily routine.

Depression can get to be a serious illness and may require treatment by a doctor. If you do have to see a therapist or counselor or psychiatrist or psychologist (they are specialists in treating this kind of illness) it is nothing to feel ashamed or upset about. It doesn't mean you are "crazy." The smartest, most talented people sometimes suffer from depression. Abraham Lincoln suffered a severe depression in his early adult life. Some well-known contemporary people who have recovered from the illness of depression include Senator Thomas Eagleton, Betty Ford (the wife of former President Ford) ex-heavyweight boxing champion Joe Louis, famous playwright Tennessee Williams, and political activist Angela Davis.

A doctor or counselor who treats emotional illness can be a good, sympathetic friend. He or she can help you understand yourself and your feelings better and help you feel better about yourself and your life.

WHEN YOU FEEL GUILTY

"I feel—well, somehow it's *my* fault they're getting a divorce. . . ."

Barbara, fourteen, is talking with her school counselor. She is able to describe the nagging feelings of guilt she has about her parents breaking up.

"Maybe if I hadn't been so ugly to Mom sometimes, or talked back to Daddy. I'd try to do better if they'd just not get a divorce. If I could just do or say the right thing, maybe the divorce wouldn't happen. . . ."

26

A lot of kids feel the way Barbara does. They think they are somehow to blame. They wish they could be better so the divorce would go away.

Kids are conditioned to feel they are somehow to blame when things go wrong around the house. They were disciplined from little children on for doing the wrong things. "No-no" is often one of the first things an infant learns. From then on, growing up is a series of guilt feelings over saying or doing the wrong things.

Kids often interpret anything bad that happens as punishment. A study was made of children who were sick in a hospital. Most of them said they thought their sickness was punishment for being bad.

Parents getting divorced is one of the worst things that can happen to a kid. The kid may feel it is a kind of punishment because he or she was bad. Of course, that really isn't the case at all.

Having a conscience and learning to feel guilty about doing wrong is a way civilized people have of developing a value system. It's the way we bind ourselves to a sense of moral obligation. That's how we can live in a complex, civilized society and respect the rights of others. We're trained to feel guilty about hurting a neighbor and stealing from him or her, so we don't do it. Some criminals don't have a conscience.

But an over-active conscience can sometimes make guilt feelings spill over into areas where you don't really need to feel guilty. You have no real cause to feel guilty over your parents' fighting. The problems your parents are having are their problems. They are grown-up problems. No kid is to blame when his or her parents get a divorce. The divorce is not punishment for something the kid did wrong.

Changing your behavior is not going to make the trouble between your parents go away.

Sometimes the anger a kid feels comes after trying very hard to be "good" so the parents won't divorce, and they get a divorce anyway.

"I tried so hard," Tim, a boy of twelve, said bitterly. "I studied hard and kept my room clean. I didn't talk back. But they went ahead and divorced anyway." Tim was angry at his parents. He hated them for letting him down this way after trying his best to be good and doing everything just right.

Sometimes parents drag their kids into their problems. For example, they blame each other for poor grades the kid made, or trouble the kid got into. Or one parent may threaten the other with, "If it wasn't for our son (or daughter) I'd leave you!"

Overhearing things like that can make you feel that you're somehow involved in your parents' fights. Or it might make you feel that you're the cause of their trouble. But that's not really the case. When parents fight, they probably want to hurt one another. Using the kids is one of the weapons they employ.

If you are able to talk honestly with one or both of your parents, you need to tell them about your feelings. Don't talk in anger or high emotion, but gently and sensibly. They can make you feel better and explain that you have nothing to do with the trouble in their marriage.

Look at it this way: One day a man was standing on a street corner, minding his business. Two cars collided on the street in front of him, jumped the curb and knocked him flat. The wreck was not his fault; he had only been an innocent bystander. Nothing he could have done would have prevented the collision. But he wound up in the hospital anyway.

When parents divorce, their children are innocent bystanders. They were not to blame for the wreck of their parents' marriage. Nothing they could have done would have prevented the wreck. But some of them get hurt emotionally.

But it's good to know you can recover. And children can

even gain from the experience. When a person lives through a bad time in his or her life, it can make that person more sympathetic, kinder, and more compassionate toward others. A kid can learn to understand his or her own feelings better and how to deal with them. He or she can become more adult, more independent.

WHEN YOU FEEL LONELY

Tony was scared. This was the worst moment of his life.

His hands felt clammy. His mouth was dry. His brain was spinning.

The police had brought him to the city juvenile shelter a half-hour ago. Then they'd called his parents. It was after midnight. His father was standing beside him now, looking grim. His mother had come, too. As usual, all she could do was look helpless and weepy.

The officer in charge told Tony's parents they could take him home tonight, but they'd have to bring him to juvenile court the next day.

In the car, Tony's father gripped the steering wheel angrily. "What has gotten into you?" he raged. "How could you get mixed up with a gang of kids like that?"

Both Tony's parents lit into him, his father with angry, accusing words, his mother sobbing.

Tony just sat huddled in a corner of the front seat, withdrawn and miserable. They wanted to know what was the matter with him! Why didn't they ask themselves, he thought bitterly? Why did they fight all the time? Why were they going to get a divorce? Why couldn't he have a nice home like other kids?

His parents had failed at their marriage. They'd failed him as parents. His home wasn't worth much. Tony didn't feel as if he was worth much, either.

Now his parents were jumping all over him because he'd

shamed them and caused all this trouble. Well, it was the first time they'd even noticed him in months. They were so involved with their own trouble the past six months, they'd hardly known he was alive. His mother spent most of her time in her room crying. His father stayed away from the house a lot. When he came home, he was grim and preoccupied. He barely spoke to Tony. Tony felt a lonely ache inside when he saw other boys with their fathers.

Most of the time Tony felt desperately alone and unloved.

Now his father was chewing him out for getting involved with the gang of kids who got in this trouble. "That's a lousy bunch of friends you have been hanging around with. Why couldn't you make decent friends?" his father demanded.

Decent friends? Tony knew what his father meant—the top school crowd, the kids who counted for something, the ones who made good grades, belonged to school organizations, got invited to parties.

Well, you had to have something going for yourself to make friends like that. You had to feel sure of yourself. Tony figured he wasn't good enough for that crowd. He had a pretty low opinion of himself. He felt like an outsider.

Not that he didn't want friends. He was so lonely; he wanted somebody to like him and accept him.

Some kids at school did show an interest in him. Like himself, they were on the fringe of things, kind of outsiders or outcasts. They'd been in trouble with the teachers and with juvenile authorities. But the important thing to Tony was that they accepted him and liked him. So he went along with whatever they did, even though his better sense told him maybe he shouldn't.

Tonight they'd gone riding in one of the older kids' van. They'd smoked pot and tried to steal a CB radio from a car in a parking lot. The police caught them, and now Tony was in a lot of trouble.

If a young person's needs to be loved and accepted are not fulfilled at home, that person will try to have those needs fulfilled outside the home, with friends who will accept him or her. An individual feeling deserted and unloved is going to reach out to whoever is there. Often, a kid like Tony will need to be accepted so badly as to make poor choices of friends to run around with.

Because of the feelings you have when you parents are getting divorced, you may need to be careful about your choice in friends. Don't allow your feelings to blind you at a time like that. Your choice in friends is one of the most important choices you can make.

EATING BAD CAN MAKE YOU FEEL BAD

What, you well may ask, has food to do with the things we're talking about? Well, your eating habits can be affected when you go through a crisis in your life, such as the one you're experiencing, and this in turn can have a considerable effect on how you feel.

If the turmoil of a divorce is going on in your home, several things may be happening to your nutritional intake. Meals at home may become skimpy or nonexistent if your parents are distraught by their marriage problems. Or everyone might be so uptight at mealtime, you don't feel like eating. Some parents seem to pick mealtime to have their battles, and that doesn't do anyone's digestion much good.

Also, when you are sad or lonely or feeling depressed, as you may be over your parents' divorce, you may comfort yourself by overindulging in candy, sodas, and cookies. Or you may substitute snacks of junk food for the regular meals you're missing.

The result of such poor eating habits is that your complexion can suffer. You might gain a lot of weight from the junk snacks you're stuffing yourself with. Your physical endurance may go downhill. Your performance in sports and schoolwork can drop. And at this point the last thing you need—along with your family problems—is to get fat and have a bad complexion, or lose weight and have no energy.

Furthermore, poor choice in the foods you eat can directly affect your emotions, doctors now believe. Not taking in an adequate supply of vitamins and minerals can make you feel depressed. It becomes a vicious cycle. You feel depressed, so you eat junk foods, and the lack of minerals and vitamins makes you feel more depressed. Your schoolwork suffers because your thinking processes are not as sharp if you're malnourished.

The general rule to follow for good nutrition is to eat a variety of foods and include each day some vegetables, fruit, milk, whole-grain cereals, and protein foods such as meat, fish, chicken, or dairy products.

But if this crisis in your family is resulting in sketchy meals at home, you may have to get by on snacks, at least to some degree. Dr. Judith J. Wurtman, a Research Associate in the Department of Nutrition and Food Sciences at MIT in Cambridge, Massachusetts, who has written several books on nutrition, made up a list of snack foods which are tasty, fun to eat, and yet supply a lot of good food value. Tacos, pizzas, submarine sandwiches, and yogurt are good, nutritious choices. Seeds of all kinds—sunflower seeds, sesame seeds, pumpkin seeds, etc.—are superb, as are nuts. They are full of minerals and a lot of the vitamins that are found also in whole-grain bread and cereals. Raisins, peanut butter, and dates are better than potato chips and cookies. For drinks, milk and fruit juices beat sodas and fruit-flavored drinks.

Cut down on your snacking, of course, if you're becoming overweight. And for added insurance it's a good idea to take a multiple vitamin-mineral tablet every day, at least while you're surviving this crisis in your life.

32

FACING UP TO THE REALITY OF YOUR PARENTS' SEPARATION

Probably a feeling shared by most kids whose parents are getting divorced, or have been divorced, is the dream that one day his or her parents will get back together. It's a sad dream —and usually a hopeless one. Tough as it is, you'll be better off to accept the fact that your parents' divorce is final. Nothing is going to change that. It sounds cold-hearted, but it is much better to be realistic. Your parents just couldn't get along. They were unhappy together or downright miserable. Either one or both wanted out of the marriage.

You'll do a lot better to put away daydreams of their getting back together and go about the business of adjusting to your new life with your parents divorced.

Not all kids are torn up by their parents' divorce. When his parents told Alan that they were getting a divorce, he exclaimed, "That's a relief! Why didn't you do it a long time ago?"

Alan had been fed up with the constant bickering that went on in his home. He was relieved that it would be over. Now he could live at his mother's home, enjoy her company and attention without the ugly fighting. And he could enjoy being with his dad on weekends. He'd still have both parents, but without the fighting.

It wasn't the end of the world. It was the beginning of a newer, happier life for Alan.

Why Do Parents Fight?

Kids are confused and hurt when their parents fight. The purpose of this chapter is to shed a little light on the complicated matter of why parents battle. This information may help you understand. Then it won't be so frightening. It may be a little less painful for you.

Of course, even if you do have a better idea of why your parents fight, there still is nothing much you can do to interfere. You can't patch up your parents' problems. That is something only they can deal with.

THE THINGS PARENTS FIGHT OVER

Parents fight over money, especially if one is a spend-thrift and the other is not. Or, if one parent resents it because the other doesn't earn enough money, they may fight. Relatives and in-laws are the cause of a lot of family squabbles. In some cases, parents just grow bored with each other—they fall out of love. Usually in that case, one parent has grown tired of the other, or falls in love with somebody else and wants a divorce so he or she can be free to marry the third party—the old "eternal triangle." That makes it very hard on the parent who was left behind. He or she feels rejected. One of the most devastating things in the world is to love somebody who no longer loves you in return. If that happens, you may have a seriously depressed parent on your hands. The depressed parent may do irrational things, may start drinking too much, have promiscuous love affairs, or suffer a nervous breakdown and require medical treatment.

The depressed parent may reach out to one of their children to console him or her, or want the child to fill the role of the leaving spouse.

Some people struggle through a divorce without becoming sick over it. But divorce can really knock the props out from under some parents.

Sex problems are high on the list of causes of marriage breakups. In a family life, sex between married partners can be a rich source of happiness and an expression of love. At the same time, a lot of other things occupy the couple's time and interest too, such as their children, home, careers, friends, hobbies, community affairs. But if the couple have a sex problem, it can push other things aside.

The problem might be a result of one of the parents not wanting sex. There could be lots of reasons for this. It could be a parent's emotional hang-ups about sex, going back to early childhood. Or it could simply have something to do with the parents' present life situation.

Sometimes a marriage partner doesn't stay faithful. He or she becomes involved in love affairs with another person. When the other partner finds out, there can be serious trouble often resulting in divorce.

If parents are battling and the kids can't figure out why, it might be over a sex problem. That is something parents usually don't talk about, especially to their children.

Drinking too much causes tragic family problems. If

it gets to the point that drinking becomes a sickness—in other words, the parent becomes an alcoholic—that can cause family disputes and may result in a divorce. You can read more about the problem of alcoholic parents in Chapter 5: "Real Trouble: Problem Parents, Problem Kids."

Drugs can be even more serious, especially if a parent becomes hooked on some form of illegal, hard drug. But there are other forms of drug misuse—for example, a mother who stays spaced out on tranquilizers or a father who keeps himself going on pep pills. Misuse of even prescription drugs over a period of time can change personalities. It can make the family situation so unpleasant for the other parent that he or she wants a divorce.

Some parents gamble too much. That can become an addiction like alcohol or drugs. It may be hard to stay married to a husband or wife who keeps the family constantly broke by throwing away the paycheck on horses or card games.

Some fathers are always "out with the boys," and spend very little time with their wife and children. This can become such a problem that the wife would rather get a divorce.

There are many other personality quirks that make it difficult to live with another person—unreasonable jealousy, lack of consideration, criminal behavior.

There are people you meet in everyday life who are peculiar, yet they are not in mental institutions. Some people behave in a perfectly sane manner part of the time but act a little crazy at other times. Some people have personalities with two or more sides. They seem like a different person at times. If you have a parent who behaves in a "crazy" manner at times, he or she could be a bit mentally disturbed.

Couples cite many reasons for getting divorced: nothing to talk about, no common interests, one partner wanting to stay home while the other wants friends and social contacts, one partner allowing himself or herself to become fat and unattractive.

Some divorces are the result of one or both parents suffering from a mental depression. Doctors are finding out that this emotional illness can cause many problems in a person's life. The person may not even realize he or she has this illness. Being tired, listless, and weepy can be some of the symptoms. But a mental depression can make a person act irrationally in other ways. A doctor can diagnose this illness and usually treat it successfully.

People are apt to get divorced when they start new decades in their life, around ages thirty, forty, fifty, or sixty. This is a time in a person's life when he or she looks back over the past ten years and asks, "Did I make the right choices? Would my life have been better if I'd done some things differently?" A person may feel regrets because plans and hopes didn't work out. He or she asks, "Do I want to go on like this for the next ten years?" This is a point when the person may question his or her marriage. If the person's life has been disappointing at this point, that person may blame it on his or her marriage and decide on divorce.

Some parents simply grow apart with the passing years. Their marriage has become so dull, their interests so different, they can see no reason to go on being married.

Changing sex roles in today's society is believed to be a cause in modern divorce. It used to be that the woman's place was in the home, while the husband pursued his career. These days, some wives choose to have a professional career, go back to college, or take a job. They want their husbands to take over some of the child-rearing and household duties, but the husbands can't accept the role of "house-husband." A divorce is the result.

The list of reasons why parents fight and get divorced could go on and on. It can be summed up in a word that is popular in divorce proceedings: "incompatibility." That simply means parents couldn't get along together. It covers a multitude of reasons.

PARENTS ARE INDIVIDUALS
WITH DIFFERENT NEEDS

When a couple marries, each person brings into the marriage his or her own special emotional needs, ideas, and hang-ups. When you consider how different each personality is in this world, you can understand why parents don't always get along.

Our personality and character may depend to some degree on heredity. Our genes may carry some inherent programming. More important, the way we are reared as children carries over into our adult life.

Nobody ever leaves childhood completely behind. Although they are adults, there are times when parents still behave as children. Some adults are more childish in their behavior than others. We are often not aware when the child in our makeup is telling the adult how to behave.

For example, a boy might learn that his father gives him approval only when he works hard and makes good grades. He might see his father setting an example by being a very hard worker. The boy grows up thinking his father won't love him unless he works hard.

When the boy is grown, he may become a "workalholic," one of those men who drives himself to work sixteen hours a day. He neglects his family for his business. He feels uncomfortable and anxious when he's not working hard. If you asked him why he works so hard, he might say, "I'm doing it for my family." Or, "To give my family a good standard of living." He's forgotten what happened in his childhood. But the secret child in him has not forgotten.

A girl might have grown up in a home where her father

was gone most of the time. Or, perhaps her father never showed her much affection. She grew up with the notion that there was something wrong with her. She thought she wasn't lovable. Her father didn't love her, did he?

When the girl becomes an adult, the secret child in her keeps reminding her that there isn't much about her anyone could love. She can't accept grown-up love very well from another person. And she can't give love in exchange very well. Or, she gives love indiscriminately to anyone who comes along, because in a roundabout way, she's still trying to earn her father's love. She's still trying to convince herself she can be loved.

Situations like this show that we all have what Dr. Grover C. Luoghmiller, a psychologist, calls "a certain amount of learned crazy behavior." By that he means that some of the reasons behind our behavior are not based on reality. It's somewhat like a computer programmed with mistaken information.

The father who worked such unreasonably long hours was not basing his reason for doing so on reality. Neither was the girl who thought nobody could love her; in reality, there was much about her that was lovable.

We all operate on a certain amount of "learned crazy behavior." The more we are able to see through this mistaken emotional information that sometimes makes us act the way we do, the better mental health we have. But it can be very difficult to do this. We can be controlled by strong emotions that are hard to understand.

When you put all these things together, you can see why parents do not always behave in a rational manner toward each other or toward their marriage. Parents have the stress and worry of earning a living and the responsibility of raising a family. Many rapidly changing social forces in today's world pull adults one way and the other. Under these pressures parents may sometimes revert to childish behavior. Their individual emotional needs might suit one another when they first marry, but may change as the years pass. Nobody stays the same.

PARENTS EXPECT A GREAT DEAL FROM MARRIAGE THESE DAYS

Divorce was rare in the world of our great-grandparents. Divorce was considered a dreadful scandal. A divorced woman was a social outcast. But it was not unusual for a man to have more than one wife in his lifetime, or a woman to have more than one husband. The reason was that people didn't live nearly as long then as they do now. So, if a person became a widow or widower, he or she would most likely remarry.

Life was much harder then. Except in the case of a few rich families, men worked from early dawn to late at night, six days a week. Women scrubbed clothes by hand, planted gardens, sewed, raised large families. What couples expected from marriage in those pioneer times was more practical. A wife needed a dependable husband who would keep a roof over the family and food on the table. A man wanted a strong wife who could cook, sew, keep house, tend the garden, and see to the children. Security was a big reason for getting and staying married in those days.

But in today's society people expect a great deal more from marriage. Most couples expect marriage to continue to give their lives some of the romance, happiness, and excitement they felt on their honeymoon. That's asking a lot of a relationship that goes on ten, twenty, thirty years or more. It often requires special effort from both husband and wife. If marriage doesn't live up to the romantic expectations of a couple, they might feel cheated and become bitter. Bickering and fighting may result. Finally, since divorce is much easier these days and no longer carries the social stigma it once did,

40

one or both members of the marriage might decide to call it quits and try elsewhere. If they have matured and learned some things about themselves and about life through the experience of the first marriage and the divorce, their second marriage can be quite successful.

WHAT ALL THIS MEANS TO YOU

If you grow up in a home where parents are unhappy with each other, you may have a bitter feeling about marriage. But a lot of marriages are happy. People find that a good marriage can bring more happiness and fulfillment than anything else in life.

A recent survey of a number of men who were highly successful in various businesses and professions were asked the question, "What brought you the greatest reward in life?"

By far, the largest percentage said it was not money, success, or recognition. Their greatest reward and joy in life came from their marriage and family.

You can use the experience of your parents' divorce, sad though it is, as something positive in your life. You can learn a lot about people and marriage. You'll know more about life than other kids your age. Then one day, you'll be in a better position to make a good choice in a wife or husband. You'll be better prepared to have a happy marriage and family life of your own.

CHAPTER 5

Real Trouble: Problem Parents, Problem Kids

"I think Larry's a lot of fun," said Miss Bradley, who taught English. "He's our class clown."

"I think he's a pain in the neck," retorted Mr. Davidson, the algebra teacher.

The junior high teachers were discussing a boy the kids called "Fat Larry." For some mysterious reason, Larry's women teachers all liked him. He was especially funny around them. He was helpful with his women teachers, often staying after class to carry their books or clean the blackboards. He'd even offer to wash their cars on weekends.

The men teachers didn't think Fat Larry was so great. In fact, they thought he was plain obnoxious. In their classes, his humor took on a sarcastic note. "He always has a chip on his shoulder when he gets around me," commented Mr. Davidson.

Larry's frequent trips to the snack-vending machines

kept him overweight. But that was okay. Jolly people were supposed to be fat, weren't they? As far as the other kids were concerned, he was "good, ol' funny Fat Larry." Larry had decided a way to make friends and to have his teachers notice him was to be funny.

But there were reasons why Larry got along better with his women teachers than his men teachers. He felt protective toward his women teachers. He wanted them to like him. But when he was around men teachers he felt hostile and uneasy. He made sarcastic remarks. The deep down reason for this behavior came from the way Larry's father treated Larry's mother.

One day, after school, Larry invited two of his friends to go home with him to play catch. He'd gotten a new baseball mitt he wanted to try out. As usual, Larry was cracking a joke a minute, keeping the others laughing. But when they started up the walk to Larry's front door, his whole attitude suddenly changed. His face turned pale. He began perspiring. He licked his lips. "Listen, I just remembered. I have to do something. You guys will have to come over some other time." He almost shoved his surprised friends out of his yard.

Larry had heard the sound of his father's angry voice in the house. He knew it was going to be one of those bad days. He was ashamed for his friends to find out how things were at his home. And he was scared about his father hurting his mother.

Larry was one of those unfortunate kids with a parent who became physically abusive. When Larry's father came home in an angry mood, he would throw furniture around and hit Larry's mother. Often, Larry's mother stayed in the house for days so the neighbors wouldn't see the bruises on her face.

That was the reason Larry didn't get along with his men teachers. At times he hated and feared his father—and his feelings about his father carried over to other men. One reason for his clowning was to cover up and not even admit to himself his deep down bad feelings of hurt, fear, and anger.

Larry had a really tough choice to make. At times his feeings made him want to hit his father back and protect his mother. But that would have been a poor choice because his father was a lot bigger. In a furious mood, he might have seriously hurt Larry, too.

The fighting got so bad one night that Larry was terrified his father was going to seriously injure or maybe even kill his mother.

Larry's best choice in a desperate situation like that was to run out of the house for help, to a neighbor's or relative's house and phone the police. That was not an easy choice, because for one thing the family battles would become public if the police came to Larry's home. And Larry was ashamed for his neighbors and friends to know what was happening. In addition, Larry was afraid his father might never forgive him for telling the police on him. But in a case like that where members of the family might be seriously injured, the only intelligent choice is to call for outside help.

Usually when police come out to quiet a family dispute, they don't arrest anybody unless someone has been seriously injured. They just talk to the parents and get them to calm down and promise to stop fighting.

It may be helpful for you to know that many cities now have shelters for battered wives and their children. This is a place you and your mother can go for protection if your father threatens or hits your mother. She can spend the night there and receive medical attention if necessary while your father cools down or gets sober. You can find out if your town has a place like this by asking your teacher, school counselor, or minister, or you could phone your newspaper or television station news room and ask them.

Some wives attack their husbands. A recent study by re-

44

searchers from the University of New Hampshire, the University of Delaware, and the University of Rhode Island, found that wives became violent as often as husbands. Husbands were slightly more likely to push, grab, shove, slap, beat up, and use a knife or gun. Wives had the edge in throwing things, kicking, biting, hitting with a fist or some object, and threatening with a knife or gun. In fact, in this study, in the overall violence index, the wives were somewhat more often and severely violent.

IF THERE IS A CRISIS CENTER
IN YOUR TOWN, IT CAN HELP YOU

Most cities now have a service that can be a great help to people in trouble. This service is a kind of crisis center where people can phone in for help or advice. These organizations are sometimes primarily designed to help people who are contemplating suicide. Therefore, they might have the word "suicide" in their name, such as "Suicide Prevention." But they usually branch out to offer help in any problems. They may have the word "crisis" in their name, such as "Crisis Intervention." In New York City, this kind of organization is called "Save-A-Life League." In Houston, Texas, it is called "Crisis Hot Line." Great Britain has an organization called "The Samaritans," and there is a branch of that group in the United States, in Boston.

You can ask your teacher or call your local newspaper or library or look through the telephone book to see if your community has such a program and what it is called. If you are having serious trouble at home—such as parents who might harm one another or harm you or hurt a younger brother or sister—and you don't know what to do about it, your local crisis center could be a big help to you. They will talk over your problem with you and advise you what to do.

The crisis centers are often community funded through

the United Way. Some are part of mental health centers. Most are manned by volunteer workers. When you are a bit older, eighteen or so, you may become interested in devoting some of your time as a volunteer worker in your local crisis center. Having been through family problems, you can be sympathetic to other people having serious difficulties. You've been there, so you *know*. And you will be doing your community a real service.

WHEN PARENTS HARM CHILDREN

Another boy Fat Larry's age, named Ralph, had a problem involving another kind of physical violence in his family. In his case, his mother took out her anger and frustration over her unhappy marriage on Ralph's baby brother, spanking him and hurting him out of all proportion to any discipline he really needed. Ralph remembered that his mother had treated him the same way when he was little. He was big enough now to protect himself, but he was afraid his baby brother might be seriously injured or even killed during one of his mother's rages.

Ralph's mother had a kind of illness. It is more prevalent than you might believe. Battered children are brought into hospital emergency rooms in every city of the nation. Parents blame the bruises and broken bones on a "fall" or some other unbelievable reason. When these cases are investigated, it is often discovered that it was the parents who beat or mistreated the helpless little children. Sometimes the result is a family tragedy. The child dies and the parents are tried for murder.

The frightening thing about situations like this is that the small child has nowhere to go for protection. In the privacy of the home, parents can treat a kid as they please. If parents are abusing a small child, only some kind of outside intervention can protect the child. And neighbors, unfortunately, are reluctant to interfere in another family. But people should make a report to the police if they suspect a case of child abuse. They could save a child's life.

People who are child abusers may have been mistreated by cruel parents when they were small. In turn, when they grow up, they take out their violent feelings on members of their family. The famous psychiatrist, Karl Menninger, has said, "To understand this we must consider how great and inexpressible may be the rage aroused in children by the treatment they received from their parents. Parents who whip their children should not be surprised if these children, once they attain the power and authority for doing so, take their revenge upon the next generation. In some cases this revenge spreads to include others than the helpless children."

In Ralph's case, he made a good choice when he decided to get outside help. Since his father stayed away from home most of the time and didn't seem to care, it was up to Ralph to protect his little brother.

If you have a situation like Ralph's in your home, some places you could go for help would be the police, the emergency room of a local hospital, or you could phone your local crisis or mental health center.

You are probably old enough and big enough so there isn't much direct threat to you. At your age, you can escape physical harm from abusive parents by running out of the house or asking for outside help. But it could be up to you to protect younger brothers or sisters.

There is a national organization that can help people who abuse their children. It is called "Parents Anonymous." Their national headquarters is at 2810 Artesia Boulevard, Suite F, Redondo Beach, California 90278. Most cities have a local chapter. They are listed in the telephone book under "Parents Anonymous."

If you know of a situation where a child is being abused by his or her parents, you can phone the organization Parents Anonymous, or write to them, and ask their advice. But, of course if the child is in immediate danger, you may need to call the police right away. There is a national Child Abuse Hotline, 24-hour a day, toll free number: 1-800-252-5400.

PARENTS WHO DRINK TOO MUCH

Parents who get drunk can be tough to deal with. They can cause all kinds of problems for their families and their kids. Some drinking parents become abusive and mean when they are drunk or drinking. Often these parents are victims of alcoholism, a sickness that is hard to treat unless the person really makes up his or her mind to do something about it.

You need to be sure this is really a problem with your parents before you say anything about it. Sometimes parents drink quite a bit but do not quarrel or become abusive.

One girl talked with her counselor about her problems at home. She talked about how her father drank all the time. She made it sound as if he stayed drunk and this was part of the family trouble. The counselor checked into the family situation. She found that the father did drink beer when he came home from work. But he was not an alcoholic; he did not become mean or abusive when he drank; and drinking really wasn't a problem with him. The girl had accused her father of being an alcoholic because this was a way of getting even with him for wanting to divorce her mother. The girl looked around for something to blame him with, and his beer drinking gave her the excuse to say something bad about him.

When alcoholism really is a problem in your family, it certainly is one of the big causes of fights between parents. If one parent continuously comes home drunk, the other parent may decide to get a divorce.

The organization that has helped alcoholics and their families the most through the years is "Alcoholics Anonymous."

48

"Al-Anon" is a branch of Alcoholics Anonymous that is especially for families of alcoholics. There is a subgroup called "Alateens" which could be of special interest to you, because it is for kids who have a parent or parents with a drinking problem. Alateens can be a big help if you have a problem like this in your home. You can meet with other kids who share your problems. You can learn how to cope with these special kinds of problems and how to get your life together. You would make a good choice to look up "Alcoholics Anonymous" in your phone book and ask if there is an Alateen group in your community.

It would also be a good precaution if you looked up the phone numbers of places like the police department, the crisis center, and the other organizations we mentioned, and write them down in a place you can find in a hurry. If there is a serious crisis in your family one night, when somebody might get hurt, that is no time to be fumbling through the phone book looking up numbers. If you are caught in a situation like that and need help and don't know whom to call, dial "O" for operator, tell the operator your trouble and *be sure to give your address.*

GETTING BACK AT YOUR PARENTS BY PUNISHING YOURSELF

Annette heard the policewoman come into the hospital room. But Annette did not look at her. She focused her gaze on a spot on the ceiling.

"Are you feeling any better this morning, Annette?" the policewoman asked.

Annette shrugged.

"We contacted your parents. They're flying here right away. They'll be here this afternoon."

Annette fought back her tears. She turned her face to the

wall. "Big deal," she said in a muffled voice. She thought, "I don't care if I never see them again. It's their fault. . . ."

Annette was a teenager who had lived in a small, midwestern town. She was a slender girl with large, dark eyes and dark hair that framed a pale, intensely beautiful face. Most of the kids thought she was the prettiest girl in her class. But she didn't make friends easily. She was a quiet, moody girl who kept things to herself. She rarely smiled.

Like some kids her age, Annette did not have a happy home. Finally, she became so fed up with her parents' fighting that she took some baby-sitting money she had saved and bought a one-way bus ticket to Los Angeles.

Annette had some vague notion of becoming a movie star. Instead, she got in with a crowd that used hard drugs. She danced in topless bars and begged money on the street to pay for her boyfriend's drug habit. She lived with her boyfriend in a small, dirty room. He talked her into using drugs.

Annette became sick with hepatitis, a serious liver disease that drug users sometimes get from dirty hypodermic needles. She was wandering through the streets one night, feverish and weak. A man raped her, beat her up, and threw her in an alley. The police found her bleeding and unconscious the next morning.

When kids are unhappy at home, sometimes they make the choice to run away. Sometimes when they run away, they do all kinds of things to hurt themselves, getting into drugs, prostitution, and other kinds of crime. The reason is that they're mad at their parents. They hate their parents for letting them down, for not giving them a happy home. And they turn this anger inward. In other words, they get back at their parents by hurting and degrading themselves. They may not consciously realize why they are ruining their own lives this way. Punishing one's self is a roundabout way some people have of punishing someone else. It's a form of protest.

There was certainly no joy in the life Annette had

50

chosen. She didn't realize it, but this was her way of striking back not only at her parents, but at life in general. It was like the old saying, "I'll show you. I'll go out in the garden and eat worms and die—and then you'll be sorry."

Annette almost did die. As it turned out, she did hurt her parents in a direct way. They flew to California to find their daughter in the county hospital fighting for her life. She was so thin and emaciated they hardly recognized her.

Sometimes, because their parents fight all the time and there is no love in their home, kids run away hoping to find someone to love them.

Another thing some kids will do just to get away from an unhappy home life is to get married very young. That is one of the poorest reasons for getting married. In most cases those marriages do not last.

Because they are unhappy at home, some girls become promiscuous. To them, having sex with any boy who comes along is their kind of self-destructive behavior. "What's wrong with me?" a teenage girl sobbed to her school counselor. "If a boy wants sex with me, I just can't say 'no.' I know I have a terrible reputation. And now I'm scared that I have VD."

This girl, and others like her, feel unloved and unworthy. These girls' parents are so busy hating each other, they can't give their children the attention and support and love they need at home to make them feel good about themselves. So, being hungry for love and feeling she isn't worth much, a girl will have sex with almost any boy who will pay her any attention. She might be confusing sex with love.

She hasn't made a very good choice; it doesn't make her feel any better about herself. After a long string of boys picking her up and dropping her, she feels more unworthy than ever. One of the most important things in life is to have a good opinion of yourself.

And, if the girl finds herself pregnant, then she has a whole new set of problems.

Boys and girls who are sexually active may catch VD—venereal disease—like the teenager who talked with her counselor. There are several kinds of venereal disease. They are spread by sexual contact. If you think you may have a disease like this, your only choice is to talk with your school nurse about it or see a doctor right away. You could go to your public health service in your city or talk with someone in the emergency room of a public hospital. It is not going to go away by worrying about it or trying to forget about it. And the long range effects on your health can be disastrous and in some cases even fatal. It could result in your never being able to have children.

Another way you can get answers about VD is to simply reach for your telephone. There is a national hotline that gives out information about VD. It is called "Operation Venus." The toll-free number to call is 1-800-227-8922. You don't have to tell them your name. They can give you advice, information, and tell you where to go locally for treatment.

Most of us have heard someone say, "He's his own worst enemy." There is a world of psychological truth in that observation. Often, we are our own worst enemy. That is especially true in cases of self-destructive behavior. The tragedy is that it is easy to see this pattern in other people, but tough to see it in ourselves.

People punish themselves in many ways, without consciously realizing what they are doing.

It doesn't seem reasonable that some people choose to do things that are bad for themselves. But they do.

Self-destructive behavior can take many forms. A person may gamble his or her money away. Another person may ruin his or her health with drugs or alcohol, or may drive a motorcycle recklessly. Another person may have more than his or her share of accidents.

Some people seem to fail at everything they try. They go from one job to another. They complain about bad luck fol-

52

lowing them around. Some experts in human psychology call this "the unconscious will to fail."

Other people take unnecessary chances. They drive recklessly. Or they seek the thrills of dangerous sports. These people have an unconscious "death wish," say some doctors who study human behavior.

We are familiar with the instinct of self-preservation. Self-preservation makes us fight to stay alive, to succeed, to avoid danger. We are less familiar with the dark undercurrent in our nature that runs in the opposite direction toward self-destruction. These two basic drives are often at war inside us. We may not be aware of this struggle.

The choices we make in life can be good for us. Or, if we let self-destructive impulses take over, we may choose to do things that can destroy our health, our happiness, and our chance to succeed in life. To a large extent, we make our own good luck or bad luck.

People who are happy and successful in life overcome the negative, will-to-fail element in their nature. They accentuate the positive. They are "success-oriented" or "achievement-oriented." They have a good feeling about themselves and about life. They are winners.

You might think about your own life, about the friends you are choosing, about bad feelings that make you want to do certain things, about the way your life is headed.

When you feel lonely, angry, and useless because of your unhappy home situation, you may fall into the trap of getting back at your parents and life by punishing yourself in one way or another. That would be giving in to your self-destructive impulses. You could become one of life's losers.

Knowing how people can fall into patterns of harming themselves may help you avoid messing up your life. Stop and think about the choices you are making. Avoid choices that can mean trouble for yourself now or in the future. Then you can become one of life's winners.

CHAPTER 6

The Nuts And Bolts
Of Divorce

If your parents decide to divorce, they begin what is called "divorce proceedings." That is simply a legal term for getting a divorce.

Since your future is concerned, it may help you to know in some detail the things that happen when parents go to court to be divorced or legally separated.

Sometimes parents divorce in a friendly manner. They go through the legal process of the divorce with very little fuss and trouble. They agree on how their property will be divided, with whom the children will live, and how much money the other parent will pay toward the support of the children. They part friends and continue to be friendly after the divorce. They still like each other; they just don't want to stay married.

If your parents must get a divorce, you are lucky if they can do it in a friendly manner. Unfortunately, that isn't always the case. In most divorces, parents feel some degree of bitterness toward each other. Sometimes one parent wants the divorce and the other doesn't. That can be a painful situation.

In some cases, divorce proceedings can be extremely unpleasant. There may be a court battle over such matters as child custody, property settlement, and support payments.

That's painting a gloomy picture. It usually isn't that bad. But it is better to be realistic and be prepared in case the divorce does become sticky.

Some parents make an effort to shield their children from the unpleasantness connected with the divorce. Other parents may drag their children into the middle of the dispute. One parent might try to turn the children against the other parent by saying bad things about him or her. One parent might try to blame the divorce entirely on the other. (Sometimes one parent might be entirely to blame. But usually each parent has contributed to the failure of the marriage to some degree whether they realize it or not.)

It's not unusual for a parent to try and get the kids to take sides against the other parent. *You don't have to take sides, and you can say so.* You can say, "I love you both, and I'll continue to do so. It isn't up to me to blame or forgive. I want to keep things open between us."

The trouble with placing blame is that it may seem to switch. One boy blamed his dad. Then he saw his mom acting irrationally, and he blamed her. He became confused. *He needed to know that he didn't have to blame either parent. He needed to be free to continue to give his love to both his parents, even though his dad no longer lived at home.*

When parents make the decision to get a divorce, the first thing they usually do. is hire a lawyer. Each parent might have his or her own lawyer, or they might hire one together. The reason for hiring a lawyer is because there are various legal procedures and papers that must be handled. These matters usually require the specialized knowledge of an attorney.

55

Some states have made divorce proceedings relatively simple. Occasionally a couple will try a do-it-yourself route through the divorce court without a lawyer.

SOME PARENTS GET A LEGAL SEPARATION INSTEAD OF A DIVORCE

A legal separation means the parents live in separate homes although they are still technically married. They make legal arrangements about dividing up the things they own. Mom may keep the house, the TV, and some of the money they have in the bank. Dad may get the car and the rest of the money in the bank. They also make decisions about other things. These decisions are legally binding. For example, they agree on who will be responsible for the children and where the children will live. Also, they decide on how to share expenses for raising the children. The husband may agree to help support his wife.

All these things are written up in a separation agreement, like a contract.

A legal separation is very much like a divorce, but it is not as final as a divorce. In the eyes of the law, the couple is still legally married. They are not free to marry anyone else. If they decide to end the separation and live together again, they do not have to go through another marriage ceremony to be married again.

There are various reasons why some couples decide to be legally separated instead of divorced. Their religion might forbid divorce. Or they might not be sure they want to take the final step of divorce. Instead, they try living apart under a separation agreement for a while.

These days, legal separations are not used much. Generally, when parents split up, they get a divorce.

WHAT ARE "GROUNDS FOR DIVORCE?"

When you hear someone talk about "grounds for divorce," it means the legal reason or cause for the court to grant a divorce. This varies from state to state. In earlier days, there had to be serious reasons for a divorce to be granted. One spouse had to prove that the other had been physically cruel or had deserted the family, committed adultery (that is, had sex with someone other than his or her spouse), was insane, or was a criminal, or things equally serious. In other words, one marriage partner had to prove that the other was at fault. If the other person did not want to be divorced, and he or she contested it, getting the divorce might be difficult or impossible. There had to be a court hearing or trial. The person wanting the divorce had to prove to the court's satisfaction that the other spouse had indeed been cruel or had committed adultery or was in some way unfit to live with.

A lot of story plots were based on the situation of a person being trapped in a marriage he or she couldn't escape. "My wife (or husband) refuses to give me a divorce," was a line often quoted in those stories. But, in the last few years, a great number of changes have been made in laws about divorce.

These days it is much easier to get a divorce. Most states have liberalized their divorce laws and have "no fault" divorces. One spouse merely has to go to court and tell the judge that the marriage just won't work. In legal terms they say the couple is "incompatible" or the marriage is "insupportable." And the divorce is granted. It is almost impossible for the other spouse to stop this kind of divorce. The very fact that the husband or wife has appeared in court and said they are unhappy in the marriage and want to end it is proof to the judge that the marriage is unsatisfactory. Some states grant divorces on the basis of mutual consent—that is, both parties agree that they want a divorce.

At the time we are writing this, the states that still have "fault only" grounds for divorce are Illinois, Pennsylvania, and South Dakota. Each state has its own set of legal rules and regulations. These laws may change from year to year. If you want up-to-date information about the legal grounds for divorce in your state, you can find it in the current *World Almanac* in your school or public library.

Even in states where getting a divorce is easy, there may be a waiting period. The couple may receive an "interlocutory decree," but still have to wait several weeks or months for the divorce to become final before they can legally marry again.

Also, there is a requirement that the person filing the divorce be a legal resident of the state and county where the divorce is filed—which means he or she must have lived there a certain length of time. This also varies from state to state. It can range from several weeks to several months. These days, the trend in many states is to shorten the time required to establish residency. In some states like Washington and Utah, no specific length of residency is required. You only have to prove that you do have an established place of residence or domicile in the state.

PROPERTY SETTLEMENT, ALIMONY, AND CHILD SUPPORT

Getting the divorce may be the easiest part of dissolving a marriage. The real hassles arise over what to do about property and the children.

When people are married for a while, they buy things like a home, car, stereo, TV. They may own a lot of things. They may have a bank account, rent property, and might even own a business. So, when they split up, there is a real headache over who gets what.

It makes things easy if a couple can work out an agreement before the divorce. This is called a "property settlement." Their lawyers might draw up a legal agreement which states exactly who gets the car, the house, the bank account, and so forth.

However, if the couple can't agree about splitting up their property, then it will be up to the court to make the decision.

Some states have "community property" laws. In these states, in the eyes of the law, the property of the married couple is owned jointly and equally by the husband and wife. If the couple is divorced, the court tries to divide the property equally. Community property states are: Arizona, California, New Mexico, Nevada, Idaho, Louisiana, Texas, and Washington.

In other states, courts try to make a fair and just decision about property distribution. They may consider such things as how much each spouse contributed to family assets, the financial condition of the spouse seeking alimony, duration of the marriage, the present and prospective earnings of each party, the needs of the spouse who will have custody of the kids, and so forth.

Some states have laws saying that only the property a couple accumulates while they are married can be divided. In other states property owned before marriage may also be divided in divorce settlements.

Some states have alimony laws. *Alimony* means that even after the divorce, the husband must continue to support his wife with a certain amount of money. This goes back to the days when women stayed in the home and were not able to support themselves.

Women's changing role in society these days is bringing about many new ideas regarding alimony and child support. New laws are giving women more and more equal standing with men. These days, women have entered the world of jobs and professions. Many wives are working when they get married. A wife may even be more successful and earn more money than her husband. It wouldn't make sense for the husband to pay her alimony. It might be that she would have to pay her husband alimony.

In about thirty-nine states (at the time of this writing), the courts may award alimony to either spouse. However, in many states the term "alimony" has been changed to "maintenance."

One new idea is temporary alimony or maintenance. In this case instead of the husband paying his divorced wife alimony for the rest of her life or until she marries again, he would just pay maintenance for a short period, perhaps a year or two. This would help support her while she finds a job or while she finishes college. The maintenance payments end when she is able to support herself.

Texas and Pennsylvania do not have such a thing as alimony at all.

Child support is something different from alimony. All states make some provision for child support. That is something which affects you very directly.

While your parents were married, you probably didn't think much about the money it took to feed you and provide a home for you to live in. It's natural for most kids to take those things for granted.

But now that your parents are being divorced, you may be worried about your future. If your dad won't be at home any longer, will there be enough money? Who is going to buy your school clothes? Who will pay the doctor when you are sick? Will you be able to go to college?

It may make you feel better to know that your parents and the courts are concerned about these things. One of the important matters that are decided in a divorce is how you will be taken care of financially. The money for your financial care is called "child support."

Some parents may come to an agreement about the

amount of the child support, somewhat in the manner that they decided about dividing their property. Your dad may agree: "I will pay so much out of my salary each week to help support the kids." Usually, the court sets the amount of child support.

Some states have laws that give specific rules to go by when the courts decide how much either or both parents will contribute to the support of the children. Some examples of these criteria are: the financial resources of the child; the financial resources of the parent who gets custody; the standard of living the child would have enjoyed if the marriage had not been dissolved; the physical and emotional condition of the child; the child's educational needs; the financial resources and needs of the parent who does not have custody of the children.

The court takes things like the above list into consideration. Then the judge tells one or both of your parents, "Well, you can afford to pay this much in child support," and he or she sets a figure. Usually, the money is paid each week or month. For example, if you live with your mother after the divorce, your father will give her a certain sum of money each week or each month. The money is to be used for the expenses of raising and taking care of you.

In the past, it was almost always the father who made the child-support payments. But with today's equal rights movement that too is changing. Since 1970, about thirty-two states have declared that child support is the obligation of both parents, rather than primarily the obligation of the father.

In some cases, the judge might decide that the mother is earning a bigger salary than the father, and therefore she should be the one to make child-support payments. Recently, in Texas, a mother was sent to jail because she wouldn't make child-support payments! Her ex-husband was partially disabled and couldn't work regularly, but the kids lived with him. Since the wife was able to earn a steady income, the judge declared she would be the one to make the child-support payments. When she refused, the judge put her in jail.

There are strict laws about child support. One parent can have the other parent arrested and put in jail for failure to pay child support.

It used to be that if a father wanted to get out of paying child support, he would go to another state. Once he crossed the state line, it became difficult if not impossible to have him arrested and brought back to his home state. But now many states have adopted a uniform reciprocal enforcement of the support act. These states cooperate in arresting and extraditing persons who fail to make support payments. A parent who lived in Texas might move to California. If he or she fails to keep up child-support payments, the authorities in Texas contact law-enforcement people in California. The California authorities can apprehend the parent and turn him over to Texas courts.

Unfortunately, this process doesn't always work as it should. If law-enforcement agencies are careless or overworked, they might not try very hard to locate the missing parent.

Most parents feel responsible about making their child-support payments on time. Some parents, however, will try anything to get out of making support payments. One girl's father moved out of the state after the divorce. He changed his name. Nobody could find him. There was no way the girl's mother could get the child support.

That made the girl feel pretty awful. She thought, "My father doesn't give a hoot about me. He doesn't love me or care what happens to me. Otherwise, why would he run out on me like this?"

The next thing, she was thinking to herself, "I must not be worth much. If my own parent doesn't love me or care about me, there must be something wrong with me. Nobody else could love me. I don't love myself."

If something like that happens to you, you can't be sure

62

your parent doesn't love you in his or her own way. No one can be certain what goes on in another person's heart.

But the important thing is not to blame yourself, or think there is something wrong with you. There are many lovable things about yourself. You will find many people in life who will like you a lot—your teachers, your friends, your minister. If you have religious faith, you have the comfort of knowing that God loves you. And later on, your sweetheart, wife, or husband will love you.

If you want other people to like you, you need to like yourself. Make a list of your good qualities. We all have some faults, of course. We can all stand some improving. It doesn't pay to be too smug. But overall you're a pretty terrific person. And it's nice to know you are unique. There is no one else in the world exactly like you.

THE AMOUNT OF CHILD-SUPPORT PAYMENTS CAN BE CHANGED

One boy lived with his mother after the divorce. They were barely getting by. One day, the boy's mother said, "I am going to ask the judge for larger child-support payments."

The boy's mother talked with her lawyer. They went to the judge. The boy's father and his lawyer also talked with the judge. The judge wanted to know how much money the boy's father was earning. He had gotten several raises in his salary since the divorce. "I think you can afford to pay more in child support now," the judge decided, and the payments were increased.

In another case, a father fell sick and lost his job. He had to take a part-time job. He explained his problem to the court. The judge lowered the child support the father was paying.

So, parents can go back to court from time to time and ask to have child-support payments made bigger or smaller, depending on the situation.

CHILD CUSTODY—
OR WHO WILL YOU LIVE WITH?

One of the biggest and sometimes most painful decisions in a divorce is which parent keeps the children. Again, this is a decision that affects you directly.

Traditionally, after a divorce, children stay with their mother. This has generally been the case if the children are very young.

With the new anti-bias sex laws, however, and our changing society, these days the father is sometimes granted custody. The parent who is granted custody is the one who keeps the children. They live with this parent most of the time.

The other parent is given visitation privileges. That means he or she can visit the children at certain times, or the children can go stay with that parent for a while. These visitation times may be on weekends or for several weeks in the summer or other holidays. The court tries to arrange visitation in a way that is best for everyone concerned.

A recent interesting development in some states, is the granting of visitation rights to grandparents.

States used to hold to the doctrine that grandparents could not visit their grandchildren if the parent who had custody objected. But that rule is changing. At this time the following states permit visitation rights for grandparents: Arkansas, California, Connecticut, Florida, Georgia, Hawaii, Idaho, Iowa, Louisiana, Michigan, Minnesota, Missouri, New Jersey, New York, Ohio, Oklahoma, Texas, and Wisconsin.

Laws in these states may read something like this: "The court may grant reasonable visitation rights to either the maternal or paternal grandparents of the child and issue any necessary orders to enforce said decree."

As far as you are concerned, the important thing to know about "visitation rights" is that no matter how bitter your parents may be toward each other, in all probability, you will continue to see both your parents, though you may see them at different times. And, very likely, you will continue to enjoy visiting your grandparents, too.

You can read more about the matter of visitation and some of its problems in the chapter "Visiting Your 'Other' Parent."

JOINT CUSTODY

There has been a new trend in some states to give divorcing parents "joint custody" of the children. Then, instead of one parent taking over all the responsibility of raising the children, both divorced parents share the responsibility more or less equally. The children may divide their time between the parents. The parents, though divorced and living apart, share decisions about the children's lives—their schooling, medical care, church, clothes, etc.

Obviously, it helps if divorced parents are on friendly terms. For joint custody to work smoothly, it is best if parents can put aside their personal differences so they can cooperate and agree about what is best for the children. It is good if they are able to communicate even though they live apart and may marry someone else.

However, some divorced parents have been able to handle a joint custody arrangement successfully even if they don't get along well and don't even speak to one another.

There are many good things about joint custody. It is an arrangement all divorcing parents should consider. Studies have shown that children get along better after divorce if they have free access to both parents. In joint custody not all the burden of raising the children is placed on one parent. And divorced fathers get to play a more important role in their children's lives, since in most cases of sole custody, the mother gets the kids.

Some attorneys and law professors think joint custody is not such a good idea. Doris Jonas Freed, J.S.D., a New

York City attorney and Henry H. Foster, Jr., a law professor, writing in the *Family Law Reporter* say that for joint custody to work, there must be full parental cooperation with a fixed dedication to the child's welfare. They say that is asking a lot of two people who couldn't get along before the divorce!

On the other side of the fence are family counselors and psychologists who believe joint custody is the best arrangement for all concerned. They say it can work even if divorced parents don't like each other, so long as they want what is best for the kids.

Mel Roman, a psychology professor and William Haddad, former associate director of the Peace Corps have written a book about joint custody, *The Disposable Parent.* Roman and Haddad believe that divorce is not the death or end of a family, but rather a reorganization of a family. They believe that divorced parents who have joint custody tend to squabble less over matters of visitation and child support, and the children are happier.

In cases of joint custody, the children may spend one week at the home of their mother and a week at the home of their father. Or they might live in each household half a week. In some cases, the children live with their mother during the school week and with their father on weekends and during vacation seasons. Each family must work out a schedule that best fits their needs.

It is best if parents having joint custody of their children live close enough to each other so the children can stay in the same school system and keep the same friends. But, says Dr. Roman, some divorced parents who live in widely separated parts of the country have worked out successful joint custody arrangements. Their kids spend part of the year with one parent and part of the year with the other parent.

Joint custody is one of the more modern ideas in divorce situations. It is well for parents to consider this option. A good, practical book on the subject is Miriam Galper's *Co-*

Parenting, published by Running Press. You might suggest to your parents that they read the book. It explains a lot about how joint custody works.

In some cases when the divorce is granted there is no problem about who gets the kids. The parents have worked this out between themselves along with how the property will be divided. But in other cases, child custody can be a real hassle. Parents may fight over the kids in court. Occasionally even grandparents or other relatives get into the act and try to win custody of the children.

New custody laws approved by various state legislatures set certain standards for courts to go by in deciding who gets custody of the kids. Some of the things taken into consideration by the judge are:

1. The age and sex of the child;
2. Who the child wishes to live with;
3. How the child relates with and gets along with his parent or parents, his brothers and sisters, and other persons involved;
4. The child's adjustment to home, school, and community;
5. The mental and physical health of all parties involved.

Guidelines such as these are to be found in the laws of Arizona, Delaware, the District of Columbia, Florida, Illinois, Indiana, Kentucky, Louisiana, Michigan, Minnesota, Missouri, Montana, Nebraska, Ohio, Vermont, and a number of other states.

The chapter, "Who Gets Custody—And What it Means to You," tells you more about the matter of custody.

You will probably stay home while your parents go about the business of hiring a lawyer and taking care of the legal matters of the divorce. So you won't be directly involved in the court proceedings.

It is possible, however, that the judge will want to talk to you to help him decide with whom you should live. You don't need to feel nervous or frightened. You won't be put on the witness stand and cross-examined the way it's done in TV lawyer dramas. Most judges are kind and considerate toward kids in this situation. The judge will probably have a private chat with you in his chambers or office room. He understands how tough this is on you. He just wants you to help him decide whether you'd be happier living with your father or with your mother. You can feel free to tell him exactly how you feel. The older you are, probably the more you'll have to say about choosing the parent with whom you'll spent most of your time.

YOUR FEELINGS DURING THE DIVORCE

The thing that you have been dreading for months or years is finally happening. Your parents are being divorced. No longer can you hope it won't happen or try to hide from thinking about it. It's real now. How do you feel about it?

During the divorce, you may hear some ugly things about your parents. Your father may say things about your mother —that she was seeing another man or spending money foolishly. You might hear your mother say that your father threw money away gambling or that he drank too much or had a lot of girlfriends or was cruel to her.

Things like that are hard to take. All the years you were growing up, you wanted to admire your parents. Your father was a hero to you. He was smart enough and strong enough to handle any situation. Your mother was good and kind and her heart was pure.

It makes you a little sick to hear such low-down things about them. But it may help you to understand that those things may be exaggerated out of all proportion. Or they may not be true at all. When parents divorce, they often want to blame the marriage failure on the other spouse. If they can blame the other person, they don't feel so guilty themselves.

You might even hear some very personal things about your parents' private sex lives. That might make you feel ashamed and angry.

During a divorce, parents sometimes tell their troubles to a friend or relative. One girl came home from school and heard her mother in the kitchen talking to the girl's grandmother. Her mother was crying and telling the grandmother private, sexual things.

Another girl heard her mother telling a close friend some of the intimate details of her marriage problems.

Some kids hear it directly from their parents. During the divorce these parents lean on their kids. They talk about personal things.

You just wish such things would be kept private.

You might feel let down by your parents. If you can't admire them and respect them the way you used to, you won't feel good about them. And then you won't feel good about yourself.

The way you feel about your parents has a great deal to do with the way you feel about yourself. You may think that there is something wrong with your parents. They are not normal. They are not like your friends' parents who stay married and get along fine. And you think if there is something wrong with your parents, there must be something wrong with you, too.

It may help you to know that perfectly healthy, normal, wholesome people sometimes get divorced. Because there was something wrong with their marriage doesn't mean there was something wrong with them as people. If they act nervous or childish or unreasonable during the divorce it is only because they are going through a painful emotional crisis in their lives. They are under a great strain.

One girl was adopted. She felt extra angry when her adopted parents fought and got a divorce. She demanded, "Why me? Why did they pick me and then put me through this ugly mess?" She hated her adopted parents for a while. Finally, she understood that they really couldn't help the situation. She learned that she couldn't rely on her parents to provide her with all of her happiness. She had to learn to rely on herself.

A lot of kids deny they have any feelings about the divorce. When feelings hurt too much, it becomes hard to face them. You may think it is easier to turn off that part of your mind.

These kids go around acting as if nothing was happening at home. If you ask them how they feel, they just shrug and won't talk about it.

The trouble is, you don't really turn the feelings off. You just shove them into a back part of your mind. But they are still there, festering and fuming. And they can make you feel bad in a lot of ways.

Some kids were asked to write down the things they felt during their parents' divorce. Here are some of the words they used: "sad;" "mad at my parents;" "mad at my father;" "mad at my mother;" "hated them;" "wanted to cry all the time;" "disappointed;" "scared-frightened;" "ashamed;" "felt sorry for my parents;" "lonely;" "felt alone and scared;" "felt dumb;" "felt I was to blame;" "wished I'd wake up and find out it was a dream;" "wanted to run away;" "ashamed at school."

There are two things kids seem to feel most when their parents divorce. Kids feel they are somehow to blame—that they ought to do something to make things all right again. And the second thing is that they stop feeling good about themselves.

In Chapter 3 we talked about what to do about your feelings when your parents are fighting all the time. Those same things can help you get through the divorce.

It may help you to think about "choice awareness." It

may help you to remind yourself that in most of life's situations you can make a choice. Most of us don't stop to think about making a choice.

You may just go along feeling bad and not even think about making a choice. You may try to put the divorce out of your mind. You may refuse to admit to yourself that your parents are really divorcing, or that you have any feelings about it. Or you may have all kinds of terrible feelings inside. And you just keep them bottled up.

You might say to yourself, "Hey, wait a minute. I have a choice. When I get so mad inside, I can run around the block, or hit a tennis ball or go out for boxing or football or wrestling in school. My P.E. teacher is real nice. I could talk to him about how lousy things are at home. He'd understand. Or I could talk about it with Tommy. His parents are getting divorced, too. I bet he'd understand. He probably feels lousy too. It would feel good to get my feelings out and talk about them with someone who understands. It would be a lot better than just sitting around moping and feeling bad inside."

To help ease those lonely, hurt feelings, you may find comfort with friends and relatives who love you.

Somehow, you will get through the dark, unhappy period when your parents are divorcing. Then you will begin a new life. There is something about a beginning that is good. It always has a built-in promise that things can get better.

YOUR PARENTS' FEELINGS
DURING THE DIVORCE

Your parents are having their own strong feelings during the divorce. Most parents feel guilty. They feel they have failed at their marriage. They feel they are letting their children down and causing their children pain.

Most parents are ashamed. Even though divorce is not

looked down on by society as it used to be, couples still feel embarrassed when they have to tell their friends and their relatives that they are getting a divorce.

Parents are often angry. They may be angry with their spouse if they feel their wife or husband, as the case may be, caused the divorce. If their spouse wanted a divorce to marry another person, they are very bitter toward that person who broke up their marriage.

Many parents become depressed. When a marriage ends, it is like a death.

Parents feel as if they have lost a part of themselves. When a couple has been married for a while, their lives become so entwined they are like one. When they are pulled apart, a wife or husband may say, "I feel I'm missing my arms or legs, or a part of me is gone."

Parents feel regrets. Even if the marriage ends in divorce, many parents remember some good times they once had with their spouse. They grieve over the sad way things turned out.

Parents are worried about the future. "How will I live as a single parent? Will I see my kids? Will I be able to take care of my kids by myself? Can I get a job? Will I have enough money? Will I be lonely? Am I doing the right thing?"

It may be good for you to understand the feelings your parents are having. If they are nervous and hard to get along with during this time, you'll know it is because of the many mixed-up and painful feelings they are having.

GLOSSARY OF TERMS

Alimony. A sum of money paid by one spouse to another for financial support, after they divorce. It is usually paid on a regular monthly basis. The amount of alimony payments may be arrived at by agreement between the divorcing parties, or may be set by the court.

72

Child Support. A certain sum of money paid by one parent to help cover the expense of raising the children. The amount of child support is set by the court and is usually made in weekly or monthly payments.

Common-law marriages. Some states have a law that if a man and woman who don't have a marriage license have been living together openly for a period of time, they are legally considered married.

Community property. Some states consider the things a married couple owns—their home, car, TV set, bank account, etc.—to belong to them in common, or jointly. In case of a divorce, these belongings are divided equally between husband and wife, unless they have agreed otherwise.

Cruelty. Conduct by one spouse which is harmful physically or mentally to the other spouse. In many states this is serious grounds for divorce.

Custody. When husband and wife divorce, the court decides that one of them will become full guardian of the children. This parent is said to have custody or responsibility in the care and keeping of the children.

Court. A legal entity set up by the county, state, or federal government to give verdicts in legal matters. Some states have "family" courts or "domestic relations" courts to handle matters of divorce. "The court" sometimes refers to the judge who is in charge and who makes the decisions about the divorce, alimony, property, child custody, and so on.

Desertion. When one parent runs away or abandons the family. This is usually grounds for divorce.

Interlocutory decree. This means the divorce has been granted by the court, but there is a waiting period of several weeks or months before the divorce becomes final. Until it is final, the couple remain legally married.

Legal separation. A couple goes to court to make legal arrangements to live apart. Their property is divided and custody and responsibility for the children is legally established by the court. However, their marriage is not dissolved by a divorce decree. Although they may live apart, they are still legally married. Sometimes parents try a period of legal separation before deciding about the finality of divorce.

Property settlement. An agreement between a divorcing husband and wife about how their belongings will be divided. Sometimes the court makes this decision.

Spouse. A married partner. It can mean the husband or the wife.

Visitation rights. The legal right of a divorced parent to visit his children. The times that the divorced parent spends with his or her children are usually set by the court. The court tries to arrange these visitation times in a way that will be best for the divorced parents and the children.

Who Gets Custody-
And What It Means To You

The things about the divorce that affect your new life the most are child custody, child support and visitation privileges.

Custody is important to you because this determines who you will live with most of the time until you are of legal age. This parent will make the day-to-day decisions in your life: when you should go to the dentist, whether you can go on a school trip, how much you should study, what your allowance will be, and so forth.

Rules and regulations about child custody can vary from state to state. In many cases, the parent getting custody has complete legal say-so about the child. The other parent has the right to visit on certain days, but has no other legal rights in the child's life, even if he or she is paying child support. In some cases, both parents are responsible. Sometimes, as we said, a judge gives joint custody. The parents share legal control of the child's life. But usually the responsibility goes to the parent you will live with.

Do you have any choice about which one will be your full time parent?

That depends.

When some parents decide to get a divorce, they discuss matters with the children. The whole family makes the decision. In that case, you may have quite a bit to say about which parent you'll live with.

You may have some pretty definite ideas about the matter, but your parents haven't consulted you. Then at least you can make your wishes known to them. If you think you'd be happier and get along better living with a certain parent, you can say so. Plan to do it in a way that is pleasant and doesn't hurt anyone's feelings. Remember at a time like this your parents may be very sensitive and nervous.

Try to make your wishes known without running either parent down. Put it in terms of how you feel. "I think I'd like to live most of the time with Mom." Or, "If I have a choice, I'd like to stay with Dad."

Whatever your feelings are, you are going to have to live where the court and your parents decide. So you may have to try to make the best of the situation.

Usually, after a divorce, children live with their mother. Less than ten percent live with their fathers. But sometimes fathers do get custody.

When Tim's parents divorced, his mother did not want the responsibility of raising Tim and his little brother, Mark. She felt it was too much responsibility for a single woman. Besides, she wanted to be alone for a while to start a new life. She wanted to go back to college to finish getting her degree, and then find a job. She couldn't do all that if she was tied down to raising two boys. So she agreed that Tim and Mark would move in with their father.

In the case of Becky, she and her sisters and brothers split up. She and her sister, Evelyn, went to live with her

76

mother. Her brother, Jimmy, and her older sister, Margaret, went to live with her father. Everyone was satisfied with the arrangement. The kids were with the parent with whom they got along best.

Sammy had been living with his grandparents before the divorce. His father was an alcoholic. His mother was seeing a lot of men and was hardly ever home. At the divorce hearing, Sammy's grandparents asked the judge to give them custody. That was okay with Sammy. He liked living with his grandparents. They had a big, comfortable home. He had his own room. He loved his parents, but he was afraid of his father when he was drinking. His mother never had time for him. She lived in a tiny, cluttered apartment and was gone a lot of the time on dates with different men.

In Sarah's case she wanted to live with her mother, and her mother wanted her. But the divorce was such a strain Sarah's mother had a nervous breakdown and had to be in and out of a hospital for nearly a year. She wasn't physically or economically able to take care of Sarah. Sarah's father traveled all the time because of his job, so he couldn't raise Sarah. So the court gave temporary custody to Sarah's aunt. After a year, Sarah's mother recovered her health. Then the court gave her permanent custody.

Adjusting to the new life wasn't quite so hard for Christina. After the divorce, she went right on living in her same home and going to the same school. The only difference was that her father moved out. She missed him and cried herself to sleep because the good, secure feeling of having her father in the house was gone. But she was comforted by the familiar surroundings—her own room, the TV set she got for Christmas last year, her clothes and books, and the pictures on the dresser. And her close friend, Becky, lived just down the block. It's a big help to have this kind of security.

The adjustment was harder for thirteen-year-old Nancy.

After the divorce, her mother decided to sell everything they owned, move all the way across the country to be near Nancy's grandparents, and start a new life.

Nancy felt scared and shy at the new school. She was self-conscious about having divorced parents. She had trouble making friends. She couldn't concentrate on her lessons. She missed her father. Fortunately, she made friends with a sympathetic teacher who sensed Nancy was having personal problems. The teacher gave Nancy extra help with her lessons and got her involved in working on the staff of the school newspaper. In time, Nancy started making friends. She came out of her shell.

If the divorce means a major change in your life like moving away from your old home, there isn't much you can do except go along with your parent. But you have the choice of looking at the positive side of the situation. A trip to a new home can be exciting. You can look on it as an adventure. You may make great new friends.

Find out all the interesting things you can about the area where you are going. Are there dude ranches in the area? Is there an old battlefield nearby or an Indian village? Will there be mountains for skiing in the winter, or a seashore where you can surf and meet kids on the beach? Will it be a big city where you can go to plays, concerts, zoos? Or a small town where it is easy to make friends? There are great possibilities for adventure and fun in nearly any part of the country.

Some parents who have a friendly divorce may continue to share, to some degree, the problems of parenthood. Donnie lived with his mother after the divorce, but she called his father several times a week to discuss things about Donnie—his school work, whether to buy him a new suit, if it was okay for him to go to a certain rock concert. One night Donnie woke up with an attack of appendicitis. His father rushed right over.

Unfortunately many divorced parents are not on such

friendly terms. Mary's parents hated each other. They never spoke unless it was through their lawyers. Her mother resented the time Mary spent visiting her father. And her father resented losing control over the way she was brought up.

How will you feel about one-parent custody?

It may take some getting used to, having one parent running the whole show. You might feel angry at times, that this one parent has the entire say-so about how your life is run.

It may have been easier, when your parents were living together, to talk one of your parents into letting you do something the other was against. For example, one parent may have been more lenient about certain things than the other. You could say, "Well, father (or mother) said it was okay if I went to the movies tonight."

Now one parent makes the decisions and that is final.

If you honestly feel you are being mistreated by the parent you live with, or you think that he or she is neglecting your welfare, you can talk this over with the parent you visit. This parent cannot interfere directly. But he or she does have the right to bring the matter before the court. The court can review the child custody at any time. If serious neglect or mistreatment is proven, the court might take the child custody from one parent and give it to the other, or to a relative.

One girl's mother spent most of the child-support payments on herself. She didn't buy nourishing meals for the girl. When the girl visited her father, he could see she was thin and sickly. He found out that the mother hardly ever cooked a meal at home. The girl was living on soft drinks and potato chips most of the time. The father got his lawyer to appeal to the court. The court gave custody to the father because the girl's mother was neglecting her daughter's health.

One father found out that his son was making the wrong kind of friends. The boy was mixed up with a crowd of kids that used drugs. Several of them had been arrested. The boy's mother had custody, but she was neglecting the boy. She let him do as he pleased and stay out late. She hardly ever knew where he was. She didn't supervise him properly. If that went on, the boy was headed for serious trouble. The father went to court and the court took custody from the mother and gave it to the father. The father proved he could do a better job of supervising his son.

The problems of your new life and what to do about them will be talked about in the next chapter.

Adjusting To The New Life

"One more week and school will be out!" Raul exclaimed. "Boy, I can hardly wait. Are you all set for summer camp, Doug?"

"I guess so," Doug replied uncomfortably.

"My folks gave me a new back-pack for making good grades this semester. We're going to do some overnight back-packing at camp this year, I heard."

Doug nodded miserably.

"We're going to win that ol' canoe race again, aren't we, buddy?" Raul rattled on enthusiastically. "Those other kids haven't got a chance against us. We're a team. . . ."

Doug blinked tears from his eyes. Raul was so excited he hadn't noticed how depressed Doug was acting.

Feelings of anger, disappointment and embarrassment were churning around inside Doug.

Doug was trying to think how to break the news. "The truth is, I'm not going to camp this year, Raul. You know my folks got divorced last winter. I'm living with Mom now. She told me that we can't afford summer camp this year. . . ."

THE PROBLEM OF MONEY

The divorce is over. Now you are going about the business of getting used to your new life.

You probably will be living in a single-parent home. The single-parent family is just not the same as a two-parent family.

Divorced, single parents have problems all their own. A big problem is the lack of money.

Before the divorce, your parents had the expense of running a single home. Now they have two. Your father may have to rent an apartment. He may have to buy another car if the property settlement gave the family car to your mother. On top of all that, he now has child-support payments or alimony to pay every month.

Unless your father is earning a whole lot of money, the child-support payments will not be enough for all your mother's living expenses. She has rent or mortgage payments to make, plus utility bills, food, clothing, school expenses for the kids, and medical expenses for the family. If your mother wasn't working before the divorce, she may have to get a full- or part-time job. But finances will still be tight.

You will most likely feel the pinch: smaller allowance, less money for clothes, fewer movies. You may be living in a smaller home.

This money squeeze can cause some bitter resentments all around. People become very emotional about money. Next to who gets the kids, most parents have their biggest fights over how the money is divided. After the divorce, fathers may be mad about the support or alimony payments they must make. Mothers may be resentful about not getting the support payments on time, or thinking they should be larger.

This financial squeeze may make you angry all over again. You probably are already angry at one or both of your parents. Their divorce turned your life upside down. Now you have to count pennies. You wonder, why couldn't they have stayed married instead of causing everybody all this trouble?

Nevertheless you are stuck with the situation. Once you make the choice to accept that this is how things really are, life could get better for you. You can say to yourself, "No amount of wishing or daydreaming is going to change my life back to the way it used to be." Then you can think about what choices you have to make things better for yourself.

You might be able to help your parent cut down on household expenses, and that way leave more for your allowance. For example, it costs a lot these days to hire people to do odd jobs around the house. And your single parent may be too busy to take care of everything. If you can do the yard work, wash the car, or clean the windows, your parent may be able to increase your allowance. If you are mechanical, you may be able to patch a screen, change the oil in the family car or fix the flat on your bike.

One teenager used a saw and some sandpaper to repair a sticking door. It would have cost his mother twenty dollars to have hired a carpenter to do the same job. Another teenager rented a carpet shampooing machine from the grocery store and saved a big rug cleaning bill. Another spent weekends painting the house.

Some teenagers make the choice of earning their own money to add to their allowance. Certain part-time jobs like delivering newspapers, baby-sitting, yard work, typing or washing the neighbors' cars are especially suited for teenagers. One girl had a talent for sewing and she added to her wardrobe by making some of her own school clothes.

PROBLEMS IN HOW YOU RELATE
TO YOUR SINGLE PARENT

Many young people find their relationship with their parents changed quite a bit after the divorce.

You might find that your single parent is more strict

than when you lived with both parents. That's because he or she feels twice the responsibility, having to make all the family decisions alone now.

If something bad happens to you, or you fail in school, or get in some kind of trouble, the parent you live with feels it is all his or her fault.

Some parents who get child custody are overly protective. Your parent might drive you up the wall, worrying about you all the time.

On the other hand, your single parent might be so busy with his or her new life as to let you run around pretty much on your own. Your parent may spoil you and be very permissive. He or she may treat you more like an equal than a child, and become more like a friend than a parent.

If you are a boy, especially if you are the oldest son, or an only son, and you live with your mother after the divorce, she may look to you as the man in the house. She may try to turn you into a substitute for your father. She may want to tell you her troubles, ask you to make difficult decisions for her and take her to the movies or a party the way your father used to do. She may do this even if you are no more than thirteen or fourteen years old. You become the "man" in her life.

This may be flattering to you. It may make you feel responsible and grown-up. And you may feel sorry for your mother and feel you need to protect her and do everything you can to make her happy. The trouble is, it may make you feel more grown-up than you should at your age. If it goes on too long, you may find it hard to feel comfortable with kids your own age, especially girls.

You need to make a choice between how much of yourself you can devote to your mother and how much time to give to your social life at school. You can talk with your mother about this. You can explain how important it is for a boy to have friends of both sexes his own age, and how important for you to enjoy teenage activities. You'll only be a teenager for a short while. You'll miss a lot if you pass it up.

84

If you are a girl living with your father after the divorce, you may find yourself slipping into the role of a wife. You may take over the household chores, do the cooking, and mind your younger brothers and sisters. If your father tells you he has a date one night, you may feel jealous and resentful of "the other woman."

This situation can cause problems in your own life. It can make you prematurely mature. That is, you may feel older, and out-of-step with kids your own age. What is more serious, you might feel out-of-step with yourself. You are playing a mature role on the outside, while inside there is a young teenager locked up and wanting out. In time you may come to wonder who you really are. People are healthier and happier if they have a clear sense of their own identity. That means being your own self at near your own age level, and enjoying friends and activities at that age level, too.

The really tough thing about situations like this is that your single parent may encourage your playing this mature role. These parents are lonely and look to their kids for companionship and support. Fathers can be relieved if their daughters take over running the household for them—something a lot of men aren't very good at doing. And mothers, needing a male figure in their lives, make little men and substitute husbands out of their sons.

So you may have an emotional tug of war with your parents and maybe with yourself, to maintain your teenage identity.

HOW DIVORCE AFFECTS KIDS OF DIFFERENT AGES

Your age when your parents divorce has a lot to do with how it affects your life.

Divorce does not have much effect on children under three.

However, many medical experts believe that from age

three through six, children need both parents more than at any other time. A separation at that time in a child's life could cause problems in his or her emotional development.

There is less need to have both parents if a child is six to twelve years old.

Teenagers are old enough to have an understanding of what divorce is all about and why their parents decided to get a divorce. Usually, most adolescents get along okay in a single-parent home. However, a teenager does have an important need and that is, he or she needs to have a good relationship with an older person of the same sex. Adolescents are going through a period when they are forming an independent identity. They need older people for models. It is good if this is a person who is strong and effective, someone who handles his or her role in life well, someone the kid can admire, someone the kid can go to for advice and follow the example the person sets. This person could be a teacher, counselor, friend, or relative.

A kid might turn to characters on TV or in movies for models. This may not be a very good choice. Many of the people we see on TV and in the movies these days are losers. They may have bad morals and warped ideas. More to the point, they are not real people. The problems they face and the way the problems are handled are just stories. There is a world of difference between real life and TV fiction. Real life problems can't always be magically solved in thirty minutes or an hour—with time out for commercials! Of course, some good models are seen on TV. If you admire the person and think he or she does something positive and worthwhile with their life, then that person might make a good model.

It is better, however, if you can relate to a real, live person. If you are a boy and think your dad is tops, then it may be good for you to spend as much time with him as you can. However, if you are living with your mother and don't get to see your dad much, or don't get along with him, it might be good for you to pal around with an older brother, cousin, or uncle whom you admire. Your coach at school might make a good male friend.

A girl usually does well living with her mother while she is a teenager. An older sister, aunt, or favorite teacher can be a good friend for her.

For both girls and boys living with single parents, the organizations Big Brothers and Big Sisters can be an important help. Through these organizations, children eight through sixteen make friends with an adult of their own sex. This grown-up "big brother" or "sister" is a volunteer in the community. He or she visits with the child on a regular basis, shares hobbies and outings and becomes a pal the kid can turn to for advice. Look in your phone book to see if there is a group like this in your city. The national address is Big Brothers of America, 220 Suburban Station Building, Philadelphia, Pennsylvania 19103, Phone (215) 567-2748. Big Sisters, Inc., has the same address and phone.

Teenagers sometimes have a temporary "crush" on an older person they admire a lot. This is usually a normal phase a kid goes through. It is part of admiring and wanting to be like someone who has become a hero or heroine to the teenager.

Another organization that is good for you to know about if you are living with a single parent is Parents Without Partners. A group like this can be helpful for both you and your single parent. It is made up of parents who are divorced or widowed. They get together and help each other with their problems. Since they often share the same problems, they can work out good choices together. You might mention this group to your parent. Perhaps you can find them listed in your telephone directory. They are an international organization. Their headquarters address is: International Office, Parents Without Partners, Inc., 7910 Woodmont Avenue, Suite 1000, Washington, D.C. 20014.

ADJUSTING TO CHANGES IN YOUR PARENTS

You may find your parents acting differently after the divorce. They may change jobs, go back to college, make new friends, and have new hobbies.

This may be disturbing to you. You had your parents cast in certain roles. But that has changed. Your mother may not have as much time for you. If she didn't work before, she may have a job now and be taking a night class at a local college. She even looks different. She wears her hair in another way. Her clothes look younger. She has made new friends—many of them single or divorced like herself. Your dad is trying to look younger, too. Instead of bowling on Wednesday nights, he goes to a discothèque with a lady friend.

You may resent the changes in your parents. You might think they are acting silly and wish they'd go back to being the comfortable way they were before the divorce.

Not all parents change this much, or in the way we described. But, being single again, they may feel lonely and unhappy. They would like to attract a new companion of the opposite sex. It might be just a temporary companion to see a movie with or go with to a party. Eventually, they probably hope to have a permanent companion again, a new husband or wife so they can settle down to a happy home life.

Some parents feel relieved after a divorce. They feel free. They enjoy this new freedom. They have a whole new set of hobbies and interests. They have dates and go out a lot in the evenings.

But some parents are the opposite. After a divorce, they go through a period of depression. They might cry a lot, neglect their appearance, become irritable and nervous. They might need to have medical or psychiatric care.

There isn't much you can do about these changes in

your parents except to be patient. You can understand they have been through an emotional ordeal and are trying to get used to their new life as a divorced, single parent.

We all change in some ways because of life events, while a part of us remains the same. The part of your parents that loves you has not changed.

WHEN YOUR PARENTS HAVE DATES

One of the things about your single parents' new lifestyle that might upset you is when they have dates. Your mother's new boyfriend comes by one evening to take her out to dinner. Or next time you visit your dad, he has a lady friend with him.

This business of your mother and father pairing off with new partners can be painful for you. It can give you feelings of anger, resentment, jealousy. It might even reawaken that big one—the deep down fear of separation and abandonment. You know your dad is going with a divorced lady who has children of her own. Does that mean he'll spend all his time with them and forget about you?

You might feel ashamed when your mother goes out with another man, or brings him home and they go into her room and close the door. You may have the feeling that she's being disloyal to your father. You still have that secret dream that your parents will get back together. How are they going to do that if they stray off with new partners? And you resent the time and attention the outside party gets from your parents. That means less time for you.

The family is no longer centered around you, and you feel left out.

These are perfectly normal feelings. A lot of kids in your position feel the same way.

It's easier to get used to the changes in your parents

and to the time they spend with their new friends and interests if you stay busy with your own friends and activities in your teenage circle at school.

WHEN ADULTS TRY TO FORCE YOU TO HAVE SEX WITH THEM

If you are a girl, you might have a special problem with your mother's boyfriends.

Some men, if they have the opportunity, will molest a young girl if her mother isn't around. It could be almost any man—even an uncle. One girl's mother (who was divorced) had too much to drink at a party. Her boyfriend brought her home and she passed out on the couch. The boyfriend had had a lot to drink, too. He wandered into the girl's room, got in bed with her and began kissing and touching her. The girl was terrified. She was too ashamed to tell her mother the next day. But it was such a disturbing experience that it had serious effects on the girl's life. Her schoolwork suffered. She became nervous. She was afraid of boys her own age and wouldn't have dates. She missed out on a lot of high school fun, had nightmares, and eventually had a nervous breakdown.

If you find yourself in a situation where one of your mother's boyfriends becomes overly friendly, kisses you too much, touches you in a way that embarrasses you or tries to have sex with you, you should not keep it to yourself. Embarrassing as it is, for your own protection you should tell your mother. If she doesn't do anything about it, or doesn't believe you, tell your father or another relative, teacher, or minister. Sexually molesting a child is a criminal offense, so you have a right to go to the police.

While young girls are the most likely to be molested, some men will try to do the same thing with young boys.

There are also cases where a girl's stepfather or stepbrothers try to make her have sex with them. While this doesn't happen in every family situation, it may be wise for you to know the possibility exists.

When an older person sexually molests a minor it can mean that he tried to get you to do sexual things with him. Or it could be the more serious crime of rape, which is physically forcing you to have sex with him. Even if he only uses threats or somehow coaxes you into a sexual act, it is still legally considered rape if you are a minor.

Kids don't have many defenses against adults. If a man begins to molest you, you may feel powerless to do anything. Kids have been trained to obey adults. Strangely, many kids somehow feel guilty, as if they themselves did something bad.

There is no reason for you to feel guilty. And certainly no reason to keep quiet about what is happening. This is one time when you have every right to raise a real big fuss, make lots of noise about it, and tell somebody who can help you.

Of course the best thing is to avoid getting into a situation like this. If your mother is divorced and her boyfriend has made improper advances, don't stay home alone with him if your mother isn't there. If he comes in while your single parent is away, make an excuse to go visit a friend. If it's at night and you can't leave the house, arrange to go to your room and keep the door locked. Or phone a relative or friend to come over.

Kids react in different ways to being sexually molested. To many it can be a serious, emotional event that can cause a lot of problems in their lives, especially if they keep it to themselves and brood over it. To others, it might not affect them as seriously. If you have been a victim of this kind of thing and you brood about it, or it is so painful you try not to think about it but have nightmares anyway, it would be better for you to talk to somebody about it.

Certainly, not all the men you meet, or all of your mother's boyfriends will try to molest you. Most of the men you encounter, your teachers, relatives, doctors, will be fine people. But it is wise to understand this problem can happen, and to avoid it if at all possible.

ADJUSTING TO FRIENDS AT SCHOOL

After your parents divorce, you have the problem of facing your friends at school. You may have the feeling that they are whispering about you behind your back. You may get the idea that they no longer want to associate with you. Most of this is just in your mind. You are naturally sensitive and self-conscious. You feel as if everyone is looking at you.

These days, divorce is so common probably other kids in your school crowd also have divorced parents. It no longer is the scandal it used to be.

The best thing is to go on about your school activities as if nothing had happened. If you do run into a person in your school crowd who stops being friendly because your parents are divorced, just scratch him off your list. There are plenty of other kids who will make better friends anyway.

The important thing is not to feel unworthy. If you start thinking you are not as good as the other kids because your parents are divorced, or that this has somehow marked you or made you inferior, you can get a lot of bad feelings about yourself. A better choice is to remind yourself that you are the same person. It was your parents who divorced. That was their problem, not yours. You are your own person. You have your own life.

DEALING WITH YOUR PARENTS' TUG OF WAR OVER YOU

After the divorce, some kids feel as if they were a rag doll being pulled apart by two adults. Each parent may want to be first in your life.

92

Some mothers play the "Your-father-is-a-dirty-rat" game. Or fathers play the "The-divorce-was-your-mother's-fault" game. In other words, one parent hates the other parent and wants you to hate him or her, too.

Your mother may try to brainwash you into thinking your father is a scoundrel.

Your father tells you all the things wrong with your mother.

When one parent runs the other down, whom are you to believe? The best thing is to believe yourself.

Parents are not entirely rational about each other during and after a divorce. There is no reason why you should see one parent through the other parent's eyes. They may have good reason for hating each other. But you have no reason for hating either one. They may have done terrible things to each other. But neither one did anything terrible to you. They may hate each other. But in most cases each one loves you.

It's tough when one parent tries to get you to take sides against the other. You want to be loyal to both of them. It isn't easy to stay neutral in this kind of situation. But it's best if you can stay out of these hassles. You can believe your own eyes and ears. Your mother might tell you that your father is selfish, irresponsible, and mean. But he's always been generous, kind, and loving to you—so that's all that counts as far as you're concerned. Your father may say your mother is fickle, two-timing, and a spendthrift. But as far as you're concerned, she's sweet and tender and a lot of fun.

One girl handled it this way: Her mother was saying bad things about her father and trying to get the girl to side with her against her father. The girl said, "Well, I love you and I love my father. I've always loved you both and I always will. Please don't try to get me to say something bad about somebody I love." That stopped her mom cold. And, of course, she could have handled her dad the same way.

THE PROBLEM OF HOLIDAY SEASONS

Some of the saddest times children of divorced parents have to go through are the special holidays, the Christmas season, Easter, Thanksgiving, birthdays. In our culture, we have been raised to think of those as family times. Magazines and television show the family gathered around the Christmas tree or the Thanksgiving table. What makes it worse, all your friends will be with their families. You will be with a single parent. It won't be the same as when your family was whole.

It's easy to become depressed during those times. That not only applies to children whose parents are divorced. It also holds true for many adults. Psychiatrists know they have many cases of depression to treat during the Christmas season. People remember their childhood, the happy times with their families. If they are alone, they brood, become sad and despondent.

It may help if you know in advance you are going to have a rough ordeal with your feelings during these times. People are able to cope with things better if they know about them ahead of time and make plans.

If, for example, the Christmas season is approaching, have a talk with your parents and find out exactly what their plans are. Will you spend Christmas with your mom or your dad? What plans have they made? Will they be with you, or will they be involved with their own friends part of the time? Then you can begin to make arrangements to fill the holidays with activities so you won't have time to become despondent.

One boy discovered that he wouldn't spend Christmas with either parent. His mother was leaving on her honeymoon with her new husband. His father would be out of the country on an important business trip. So the boy was shuffled off to spend Christmas with an aunt and uncle.

It could have been a miserable Christmas, but with a little planning, the boy turned it into a super success. He

94

wrote to his aunt ahead of time to find out what he could do during the holidays. He learned there was a ski resort near where his relatives lived. Great! He'd always wanted to learn to ski. He stayed so busy with his new adventure he didn't have time to let the blues get him down. And he met some neat kids at the resort.

A girl's best friend came from a large, happy family. The girl loved being at her friend's home. With all the brothers, sisters, and cousins around, it was a constant joyful confusion. No time to feel lonely there! The girl arranged to spend much of the holiday season with her friend.

Another boy was a movie fan. He saved his money and saw a lot of moving pictures during the holiday season. Going to a lot of movies might not be a healthy way to spend all your free time. But under the circumstances, it helped this boy keep his mind off his troubles during this rough time. It was an escape.

Another girl was spending the first Christmas season with her mother after the divorce. She knew it would be a sad, lonely time for both of them. Her mother was depressed. They'd both just sit around and mope. Then the girl hit on the idea of "adopting" a poor family. The girl and her mother got busy making presents, baking cookies, and planning a big Christmas dinner. On Christmas day, they invited the poor family into their home for a turkey dinner and handed out gifts under the Christmas tree. It turned out to be a warm, happy occasion for everyone.

These kids hit on ways to keep from feeling too bad during those special days, mostly by keeping busy with friends and activities to take their minds off themselves.

None of these things is going to make up entirely for not having your parents together the way they used to be. You're bound to have some rough moments when you want to go off by yourself and cry. But planning ahead can make those times less painful.

WHEN YOU FEEL ABANDONED

You may feel scared and lonely when the time comes to see your parents part for good after the divorce.

One of your parents packs up and moves out. Just the physical act of doing that is a kind of abandonment—going away and leaving you behind. You may have the unreasoning fear that when your father moves out, he'll just keep on going and you'll never see him again, or that once he's gone, he'll stop loving you. Then if something happened to your mother, you'd be left all alone.

But you'll soon find that your fears are groundless. Your father divorced your mother—he didn't divorce you. You still have two parents—they just live in different places. And they love you as much.

It's reassuring, also, to know that no matter what happens, you're not going to be abandoned. If something happened to take both your parents out of the picture, you probably have relatives who will take care of you. And the local, state, and federal governments are always ready to step in to see that kids are safely taken care of, no matter what happens.

Most kids find, after they settle down to their new life, that a feeling of security comes back. They adjust to the routine of living with one parent and visiting the other. The ugly fears of abandonment and separation fade away.

In some rare cases, one parent actually does disappear after the divorce. This happened to a girl named Margaret. She was eleven when her parents divorced. Her father moved away. Margaret heard nothing from him for many years. She didn't know if her father loved her any more. After awhile, her mother remarried. Margaret got along very well with her stepfather. But she still thought about her real father and wondered where he was and if he ever thought about her. It wasn't until she graduated from high school that she heard from her real father again. They began corresponding, and eventually Margaret went to visit him.

Margaret's real father did love her. But he was an irresponsible kind of man. He had married too young. He couldn't hold onto a job. The responsibility of making alimony and child-support payments was too much for him, so he just ran away. He had been running away from responsibility all his life. As the years passed, he matured and settled down to a regular job. Finally, he got in touch with Margaret.

Margaret's father probably couldn't help being the kind of person he was. Life sometimes gets to be more than some adults can handle. It is not a simple matter to decide if a parent loves his children if he deserts them the way Margaret's father did. No one can say for sure what is going on in a parent's mind or heart, or what life problems they face. In other cases, even though absent, in his or her heart that parent still loves you.

THE DREAM OF GETTING YOUR PARENTS BACK TOGETHER

It probably won't change your feelings much to repeat what was said in an earlier chapter—the chance of divorced parents' getting back together is remote. You'll still have that secret dream; many children of divorced parents do. But it will gradually fade as time passes. Your parents will most likely find new partners and remarry. Eventually you'll put the old dream away along with childhood memories, and you'll be happy to go on with an exciting new life the way it really is.

THE FIRST YEAR IS THE HARDEST

Studies show that on the average it takes a kid about a year to adjust to his or her parents' divorce. If your parents recently divorced and you're having a rough time of it, you can tell yourself that by the end of the first year your life will settle back to being more normal, and you'll feel a whole lot better. That's something to look forward to and hold onto when the going gets rough.

CHAPTER 9

Visiting Your "Other" Parent

"I have a big weekend planned for us, Tim. I got tickets to the game Saturday, and—"

It was pretty obvious to Tim that his dad was feeling guilty. The last two week-ends had been big disappointments to Tim. Weekends were the times he was supposed to get to visit his dad since his parents divorced. Only it hadn't worked out that way. At least not the past two weekends. At the last minute, both times, Tim's dad had called, "I'm sorry, Tim. But this big business deal I'm working on—Well, I have to fly to Atlanta, and—"

So now, he was trying to make up for the disappointments. Well, Tim thought, he was still mad about what had happened. And how could he be sure his dad wouldn't pull the "big business deal" excuse and disappoint him at the last minute again?

"I guess I can't make it this weekend, Dad," Tim interrupted. "I have this big six week's test coming up. I'm going to have to study all weekend."

"But Tim—"

They argued about it for a few minutes. Then his dad got huffy and hung up.

Tim moped around the house that weekend, feeling miserable. He didn't really have to study for a test. He'd just wanted to get back at his dad. But he sure had cut off his nose to spite his face, he thought. Now he was stuck in the house with his mom all weekend. She was thinking of a dozen chores for him to do. He was missing a chance to see the big game. But he had too much pride to call his dad back and try to patch things up.

Both Tim and his dad nursed their hurt feelings for a week until they got back on better terms.

VISITING YOUR PARENTS CAN ENTAIL PROBLEMS

According to the divorce arrangement, you live with the parent who has custody and visit the other parent on certain days. This is spelled out clearly by the court. For example, you live with Mom during the week, but you spend Saturdays with your father. Or, you live in your mother's house during the school year, but you spend summer vacations with your father.

It's boiled down to a formula. It seems simple enough. What could go wrong? Plenty.

Somehow, life and human emotions don't always obligingly follow a court order. All kinds of sticky problems can arise over this matter of visitation. But with a little clear thinking they can be solved.

The matter of visitation often requires constant renegotiation between your parents, between you and your parents, and with yourself.

It is most important, in solving problems over visitation

rights, that the lines of communication be kept open. You should feel free to talk with both parents about how you feel in regard to the visits. And your parents should be able to talk about the problems that arise and negotiate when possible. Unfortunately that doesn't always work because some parents aren't on speaking terms after the divorce.

One problem you may have is that you may find the visits awkward and strained.

For example, you spend the week with your mom in a daily life situation. You share with her all the little events that go to make up family life—who gets the bathroom first in the morning, what clothes to wear to school today, which TV shows you both want to see. Over the evening meal, you tell her about things that happened at school that day. She talks about something the neighbors did, or, if she's working, something that happened at her job. It's comfortable. It's routine.

Then, suddenly, on the weekend, you find yourself with your father for a certain number of hours. You may not know what to say to him. He lives in another world, now. You can tell that he's uncomfortable, too.

Both of you feel uptight. Your dad thinks he is obligated to show you a good time. He hauls you around to movies, zoos, museums, takes you out to dinner. He asks a bunch of dumb questions about what you're doing in school. You try to think of something to say to him. He wasn't the easiest person to talk with when he lived with your mother at home. But it was different then. It was a family situation on day-to-day terms, like with your mom now. He'd slop around in his bedroom slippers, needing a shave on weekends, and maybe yell at you to get your bike out of the driveway. You didn't feel uncomfortable and awkward with him then. You were sharing your home and daily life with him.

Now he can't even yell at you for leaving your bike in the driveway, or jump on you for not doing your homework.

Your mom has taken over all those matters of discipline. So your dad has become something of an outsider.

One way you might feel more comfortable visiting your dad is to convince him he doesn't have to knock himself out entertaining you. It might be fun for both of you if you just go over to his apartment and mess around the way you do at home. Tell him to read the paper or work on his car, or do whatever he wants to do. You'll just hang around. Maybe you could take some homework or a book to read.

The point is, just being around each other can be enough. He doesn't have to be constantly entertaining you. The two of you don't have to keep a strained conversation going. It would be nice if you could think of his place as just another part of your home. Maybe you could arrange a small corner of his apartment for some of your things that you leave there. You could have a desk with some of your books and records. If he has a big enough place, you might even have a room of your own.

One boy and his dad worked out a casual relationship like this. Sometimes the boy would bring some of his friends along on the weekend visits. His dad had a yard at his place. The boys played touch football in the yard while his dad washed his car. It was a very easy-going situation. And there were times when the boy and his father would sit around and slip into a comfortable conversation. They might decide to go to a movie, or go fishing, or watch TV. But it wasn't all carefully planned out like a bus schedule that made them feel strained. They just did what came naturally.

One girl and her parents were having a lot of trouble over her visits with her father. It so happened that her father was pretty well-off financially. After the divorce, her mother had to work to support herself. The girl lived with her mother in a modest home. According to the court ruling, the girl visited her father on Sunday afternoons. Her father, who had remarried, lived in a more elegant home. He drove a big car.

TAKING A LOOK AT THINGS THROUGH YOUR PARENTS' EYES

Most of this book is about the problems you are having that are caused by your parents' divorce. This might be a good time to take a closer look at the problems your parents are having. Having a better understanding of their side can help in ironing out problems of visitation.

If the single parent you are living with is your mom, she is probably one of the busiest people in the universe. Probably, in addition to running a household, she works at a job. In the mornings she wakes up early and rushes around to feed the kids, get them off to school, clean up the breakfast dishes, meanwhile dressing herself and fixing her face and hair so she'll look neat at her office. After putting in eight hours at her job, she hurries home to cook supper, stopping on the way to pick up some things at the grocery store. After supper she has the usual battle with the kids over getting homework done, which TV shows they can see, and trying to get them to bed. Somewhere between all that, she does the laundry, straightens the house, balances her checkbook, pays some bills, and answers the phone.

This is a normal day when something doesn't go wrong. But something always goes wrong. The car has a dead battery, the washing machine conks out, your little sister comes home with the measles, the dog has to be taken to the vet, the roof springs a leak and the hot water heater fizzles out.

When your parents were married, a lot of those problems were divided between your mom and dad. But now one person—your mom—has to do them all. And, when your father was home, once in a while, your mother could lie down in her room with a headache and know she wouldn't be disturbed. But these days a headache is a luxury she can't afford. And having a few minutes' peace by herself is out of the question.

Decisions are another thing. There used to be another

During the few hours the girl was with him, her fatl
drive her around town in the flashy car, take her
pensive restaurant, and treat her to expensive gifts.

The girl's mother was unhappy with the arra
She complained that the girl was being spoiled by h
When the girl came home from the weekend visit,
stubborn and hard to manage. She didn't want to
homework, or go to bed on time. And she complain
the plain, home-cooked meals her mother served, al
was good, nourishing food.

There was a lot of hostility between the pare
mother was jealous because she was having to struggle
ends meet, while her ex-husband, the girl's father, w
ing around a good-looking young wife and had p
money to spend. The father was mad because he l
little time with his daughter. He only had a few l
Sunday and felt he had to make every minute count.

Since the mother and father couldn't talk withou
in a bitter, name-calling argument, they had to have
selor help solve the problem. The father pointed out
had so little time with his daughter, he was treating h
date. He admitted he indulged and spoiled her.

A new visiting arrangement was worked out. In
the girl visiting her father a few hours every Sunc
would spend several days at his house on school holid
wouldn't see her father as often, but when she did go
she could actually live at his place. That way, both th
and daughter could relax. He didn't have to feel that he
entertain her every minute. They had more time to be
with each other. The father stopped spoiling her so
And the girl's hard-working mother had some time to
Everyone was satisfied with the new arrangement. A
girl's attitude improved.

Sometimes by renegotiating the visiting times, pi
can be solved.

adult to help in decision making. Should your brother have expensive braces on his teeth? The doctor says your sister should have her tonsils out. Your mom spends some sleepless nights worrying about whether it's the right thing to do. You are flunking math at school. Should you go to a different school? Now your mother has custody of the kids. The final decisions and responsibility are hers alone.

Discipline could be a problem. Your mom used to have your father in the home to back her up when she made rules. Just having two adults on the side of law and order carried more weight. It takes a certain amount of energy to take a firm stand on an issue of discipline. A single parent can get so worn down battling the kids, she feels like throwing up her hands and giving in.

Kids with a single parent are more likely to: argue over bedtime and television rules, not want to clean up their rooms, decide they don't want to do their homework, fight with their brothers and sisters, and not see why they have to come home at a certain time after a date.

And after they come back from visiting Dad, they may be even harder to manage. Since Dad only has them for a short time, he's inclined to spoil them.

Now if Dad got custody, he has all the same problems just described. Plus he's probably not very handy at keeping house. So in addition to his job, he's trying in a pretty clumsy way to cope with things like laundry, house cleaning, and preparing meals. If he knows as much about cooking as most fathers do, you're probably in for a lot of TV dinners!

In addition to all these things your single parent must cope with, there is one more that he or she probably doesn't talk about: loneliness. You wouldn't think with all that going on your parent could possibly be lonely. After all, aren't the kids around to keep your parent company? True, but no matter how much your parent loves you and your brothers and sisters, he or she is lonely for another adult. Kids and adults live in different worlds. As you know, your parents just don't understand certain things about your life. Only a kid your age understands. The same is true for the adult world. So there are times—maybe late at night after the kids are finally in bed— that your single parent will feel very sad and lonely.

If—as in most cases—your mother has custody of you and your brothers and sisters, and your father has visitation privileges, then your father has certain feelings to deal with.

For many years, as you were growing up, your father had the role of "head of the family." He was the protector and the provider. This is the traditional way most fathers feel.

Now, suddenly, your father finds he is an outsider. He has very little authority over the way your life is managed. This can be pretty tough on most fathers. He used to feel that his presence was a source of security to his wife and children. Now they get along pretty well without him.

Most fathers want to protect their children against danger. In earlier times, it was the father's strength that protected the kids from wild animals. These days, fathers want to protect their children from modern dangers—drugs, automobile accidents, the wrong kind of friends, making bad choices that can ruin their lives. But fathers can't do that if they are no longer a part of the children's daily lives.

A father also likes his kids to feel he gives them financial support. Even though he may be making child-support payments, it's not the same as bringing home the paycheck when he lived at home. To make up for this, he might buy his kids expensive gifts when they visit.

What do these feelings and problems of your single parents have to do with the problems of visiting?

The how and when of visitation can be a touchy subject between divorced parents. A lot of their problems we have described make them nervous and uptight. Perhaps you can better understand why it is sometimes difficult for divorced parents to settle these matters in a calm, reasonable way.

Your father may want to come over to your home to

pick you up. That way he can see if your mother is providing a clean, comfortable home for you. But your mother may resent having her ex-husband in her home, especially if she has remarried. And her new husband may object to the presence of her ex-husband. That can be solved by the kids going to their father's place on the bus.

Your single parent mother may remarry. Then she may move to another city with her new husband, taking the kids with her. Your father may complain that now he won't get to visit his kids on weekends. The solution is to change the visit schedule so the kids can go by bus, train or airplane to their father's place for several weeks in the summer. Your father may drive up to see the kids. Then they probably will visit him at a motel where he is staying while in their new home town.

Sometimes even though your divorced parents live in the same town, transportation can be a problem. Getting you back and forth between the two homes takes a certain amount of time and money, especially if it is a large city and there is a pretty good distance between Mom's and Dad's places.

These various problems of visiting can be worked out. But it takes a certain amount of negotiating and compromise between your parents to accomplish this. And with the feelings of resentment, hostility, jealousy, and suspicion going on between them they may not be in a mood to negotiate, much less compromise.

In that case, there is only one solution—a third party must be brought in to help solve the difficulties. This third party could be a friend or relative they both trust. It could be the family doctor or the pediatrician who becomes the mediator, especially if the children's health becomes involved in the dispute. In many cases, the parents have to contact their lawyers and go back to court so the judge can settle the visitation problem.

It is a good choice if your parents decide to go to a

trained counselor such as a psychologist, psychiatrist, or social worker who specializes in family problems. These days, more and more people are doing just that. These counselors understand human nature and human problems. They know how to deal with the hostility between divorced parents. And usually they can help find solutions and offer suggestions that can iron out the difficulties over visitation.

SOME OTHER PROBLEMS OF VISITATION

Some situations can come up that make you feel guilty. For example, you're supposed to visit your dad this weekend. But your best friend's family wants to take you along on an exciting weekend trip to the beach. You decide to call your dad and tell him you want to skip this week's visit with him so you can take the trip with your friend. Then you feel lousy on the trip because you think about how you disappointed your dad.

Sometimes it's your parent who disappoints you. All week you were looking forward to a weekend with your dad. At the last minute he calls to tell you he has to be out of town on a business trip.

These kinds of disappointments can sometimes be avoided by talking over the situation ahead of time with your parent, and making plans with him or her. For example, in the case of wanting to go to the beach with your best friend, if you explain fully to your father how important this is to you, he'll probably understand. Then you won't have to feel guilty. You and your father can perhaps plan another time together to make up for the week-end you'll miss seeing him. The same thing is true about your father's unexpected business trip. He might not know about it in time to tell you in advance. But he can talk it over with you before he leaves and perhaps plan something special with you to make up for the missed weekend.

In spite of everything, hurt feelings and disappointments

108

may happen from time to time. If they do, it's better not to keep them to yourself and brood over your hurt feelings. Bring them out into the open and talk over your feelings with your parent. Holding feelings in too long can make them worse. You might say, "Dad, I really got my feelings hurt when you went off to that golf tournament instead of spending the weekend with me like you promised."

By talking about your feelings with your parent, the two of you might have a better understanding of each other and feel closer. If you keep your feelings to yourself too much, resentment toward your parent can build up. Of course, that's true about your parent's feelings, too.

It may also help if visiting time is made somewhat flexible. Both you and your parent might feel more comfortable if visits are not on a rigid time schedule. Then if you have a school activity you'd rather go to, or your parent must take a business trip, you can arrange your visit for another weekend.

Some kids are happier if the visits are for longer periods of time and less often: for example for a long school holiday and a week or two in the summer rather than a few hours every Saturday. Others can't be comfortable with Dad for more than three or four hours at a time.

Again, these things are a matter of negotiating between your parents and between you and your parents.

Some kids find it tough going back to the routine of school and weekday living with mom after a glamorous weekend with dad. A boy named Jerry had a super dad. On weekends, with his father, Jerry did as he pleased. His dad let him stay up late, watch all the TV he wanted, and eat all the junk food his stomach would hold. His father was so anxious to have Jerry like him that he bought Jerry almost anything he wanted. And he hardly ever punished or scolded Jerry.

Naturally, when Jerry returned to his mother after a weekend like that, she had a rough time keeping him in line.

Jerry's father spoiled him so badly because he felt guilty

over the divorce. He wanted to make it up to Jerry. Also, it was something of an ego trip for Jerry's dad. He needed so much for Jerry to like him, he was trying to buy Jerry's love. But he really wasn't doing Jerry any favors. The more he spoiled Jerry, the harder it became for Jerry to live in the real world.

This is a trap many parents fall into after a divorce. They are afraid of losing their children to the other parent. It's a trap for some kids, too. It makes it easy for them to blackmail parents into getting what they want. They tell Mom, "But Dad lets me stay up and watch the late show on TV." Or, they say to Dad, "Well, Mom said I could start using eye shadow."

If the parents aren't communicating, a kid might get by with this emotional blackmail for a while.

Some parents try to pump their kids for inside information about the other parent. Dad wants to know if Mom is dating other guys, how she's spending her money, who her friends are. Mom might ask her kids—after they come home from a visit with Dad—if he's seeing a girlfriend, if he's gotten a raise at work, if he's drinking.

A good choice in a situation like that is to try and stay out of it. It won't make you feel any better about yourself to be a spy for one parent against the other.

People who are comfortable with themselves, who have a good opinion of themselves, are usually happier and more secure. Being secure with yourself, you are able to have good feelings about other people.

Taking advantage of your divorced parents, using emotional blackmail to get what you want, or acting as a spy for one parent against the other, aren't the best ways to make you feel good about yourself.

If you have brothers and sisters, this may create a special problem in visiting your dad. If you all pile in his car to go off for a weekend visit, you might be competing for his attention during the short while you're with him. Some kids are happier if they take turns visiting their father. That way, you'll have him all to yourself. But other kids like to make it a family gathering. They are happier and more comfortable if all the kids are together with Dad at the same time.

The next big adjustment in your life comes if your mom or dad get married again. Those problems will be talked about in the next chapter.

If Your Mom
or Dad Remarries
(Getting Along with Stepmother,
Stepfather, Stepbrothers, Stepsisters)

"Mom said she'd be ready in a few minutes," Benji told Mr. Wilke.

"That's fine, Benji. Say, that will give you and me a chance to talk. How's school?"

Benji squirmed uncomfortably. Why did adults *always* ask that corny question when they were trying to think of something to say to a kid? "How's school!" What did they expect a kid to say?

"Okay, I guess," Benji muttered. He wished he could escape. But his mother had given strict orders for him to stay in the living room and keep Mr. Wilke company until she finished dressing.

There wasn't anything really wrong with Mr. Wilke. Actually, he was a pretty nice guy—better than some of the men Benji's mother had dated since her divorce. The thing about it was, though, Benji could see that his mom was getting serious over Mr. Wilke. In fact, she'd been dropping some hints lately that it wouldn't be long before Mr. Wilke was going to be Benji's stepfather. Benji wasn't at all sure he liked the idea. He had mixed feelings.

He felt self-conscious around his mother's boyfriend. Mr. Wilke was trying hard to get Benji to like him. But the feeling between them was strained.

Benji was relieved when his mom came downstairs. She looked flushed and her eyes sparkled when she greeted Mr. Wilke. Benji felt embarrassed when they kissed in front of him. It looked serious all right!

Benji went up to his room. He watched out of a window as his mom and Mr. Wilke drove off.

Benji worried about the changes that would come to his life if his mom got married again. A part of Benji resented the idea of another man taking his real father's place in the home and in his mom's life. On the other hand, Mr. Wilke could be a lot of fun. And he knew a lot about sports, one of Benji's favorite subjects. Another thing Benji worried about was the fact that that Mr. Wilke had two sons close to Benji's age by a former marriage. They lived with him. So, Benji would have to share his home and life with two stepbrothers. He'd have to share his mom with them, too. He didn't think he would like that.

SECOND MARRIAGES ARE USUALLY HAPPY MARRIAGES

Four out of five people who get divorced eventually remarry. And, according to recent surveys conducted by a national opinion research center, most second marriages are successful.

Dr. Frederic F. Flach, a New York psychiatrist who is an associate clinical professor of psychiatry at Cornell University Medical College and has written a book, *A New Marriage, A New Life,* agrees that second marriages have an excellent chance for success.

In an interview, Dr. Flach told us, "People not only learn from the first marriage, they also learn a great deal from the time that they spend as a single person after the divorce. As they develop new relationships in their single life, they begin to understand certain concepts that help them have a successful second marriage. They learn that no relationship is static. They realize that people do have conflicts. They work harder to learn the art of reconciliation.

"When people enter a second marriage, they have more realistic expectations. They realize that the honeymoon excitement, however great, cannot go on forever. They understand that love will mellow and that this change in their feelings does not mean that love has died."

Dr. Norvel Glenn, a professor of sociology who has been studying second marriages, says that for most people the experience gained in an unsuccessful marriage is useful in the future. "In some cases, people realize in retrospect the mistakes in their first marriage that they don't repeat. For example, a husband who was very committed to his work may not have spent enough time with his first wife. In the second marriage, he may rearrange his schedule so that he doesn't do the same thing again.

"Or a woman who married very young, maybe even in her teens, might have picked for her husband a football star. The second time around, she may realize that the characteristics she married him for do not make a good basis for selecting a husband. Instead of looking for someone with outer charisma and a following of adoring fans, she may look for other characteristics in a mate: personal warmth, kindness, a loving, affectionate personality. These are traits which she now realizes, based on her experience with her first marriage, are relevant to marriage.

"People do learn from experience. And a broken marriage can be so traumatic that people learn a great deal about what marriage should be like.

"The high divorce rate in recent years leads many people

to believe that marriage no longer works. But that conclusion is wrong. Second marriages do work."

So, if your dad or mom is going to marry again, there is a very good chance that this time they will have a happy, successful marriage. There are no guarantees, of course. Unfortunately, some second marriages fail, too. But the odds are in favor of your parents' second marriages being good ones.

HOW YOU WILL FEEL ABOUT IT

You may have some mixed feelings of your own to deal with when Mom or Dad remarries.

If you are a boy and your mom becomes serious about a boyfriend and it looks as if they'll marry, you may have some deep, unconscious feelings of jealousy to contend with. It's normal for most boys to feel that way. And, while your mom was divorced and single, you probably felt extra protective about her. You had become the head man in your household.

If you are a girl, you may have those feelings of jealousy about your dad and his new wife.

Whether you are a boy or girl, you probably will resent an outsider coming in and taking the place of your real parent. In spite of the divorce, you think of your real Dad as your mother's husband. Now somebody else is going to be her husband, sleep in her bedroom with her, live in the house with you and your brothers and sisters, hang his toothbrush in the bathroom and his clothes in the closet. That takes some getting used to.

And this outsider is ending for good your secret dream that your parents will get back together. You're not sure if you can forgive him for that.

YOUR STEPFATHER

This guy has been dating your mother for several months. Your mother is hinting around that they might get married—trying to prepare you. The guy is knocking himself out to make you like him. He brings you presents. He's super nice to you. He's a little too nice. He makes you uncomfortable. You wish he'd back off and be a little more cool about it.

Or, it's the other way around. You're going to get a new father. You're so excited. You want desperately for him to love you. But he seems a lot more interested in your mother. He treats you okay, but he seems a lot happier when you go to your room to study so he has your mom to himself.

You may be rushing things. Give him time to get used to the idea of being your stepfather. Love and friendship take time to develop between two people. As you live under the same roof with him, sharing family times, family jokes, family problems, a closeness and affection most likely will grow between the two of you.

It's possible, of course, that he might never show you a lot of affection. A few stepfathers are like that. If so, you'll have to accept the fact that he married your mom, not you. You can fill the holes in your life with friends your own age and activities that keep you occupied.

It's important not to get demoralized if your stepfather doesn't love you. Tell yourself that no matter how great you are, not everybody in the world is going to love you. That doesn't mean anything is wrong with you.

More than likely, you are going to compare your stepfather with your real dad.

If you have a good relationship with your real father, admire him tremendously and think he's just the greatest, there is no way this new guy is going to measure up to him. You probably will think of your stepfather as second-rate. You'll resent him trying to take your father's place. And if he sides with your mother in disciplining you, or tries himself to discipline you, then you're really going to get steamed.

A girl named Suzanne was in a situation like that. She

had a real super dad. He was handsome, could play the piano, write poetry, and paint. He was charming. He always had a lot of friends. And when he took Suzanne to a restaurant, he was sophisticated and smooth. She was proud to be seen with him.

Then her mother married a rather colorless man. He wasn't as tall as Suzanne's real father, nor as handsome. He didn't have any special talents. He wasn't glamorous. And he didn't make friends easily like her real dad. He'd just putter around the house on weekends and watch TV with Suzanne's mother.

Suzanne was cool to him. She couldn't understand how her mother could marry anyone so drab after being married to a winner like her father. She was a bit embarrassed to introduce her stepfather to her friends.

Then her mother had a long talk with Suzanne. She explained that she was much happier with her second husband than she had ever been in her first marriage. This man was kind and considerate and gentle. He put Suzanne's mother first in his life. Suzanne's real father had been so busy spreading his good looks and charm around he had never given Suzanne's mother the attention and affection she needed. He had never made her feel loved.

Suzanne realized that while her real father truly was one of the greatest dads in the world, he hadn't won any prizes as a husband. She began seeing her stepfather through her mother's eyes and she realized that he did have a lot of wonderful qualities.

It can work the other way around, too. If your real father was a disappointment, if he didn't love you much, or spend time with you the way a father should, you might expect your stepfather to make up for all that. You want him to be the kind of father your real father failed to be.

If you're lucky that might happen. But you have no guarantees. Probably your mother takes into consideration how the man she plans to marry will treat you. It's not likely she'll marry someone who will mistreat you—although occasionally that does happen. But, in your mind, there is a difference between your stepfather just being reasonably decent to you, and being a real, full-time father.

If you miss the boat the second time, if your stepfather is a disappointment the way your real father was, you're going to have a struggle not to feel depressed and think there is something wrong with you. It might make you feel better to know things like that happen to other kids, too. And there is absolutely nothing wrong with the kids.

If you're a teenage girl you might find yourself competing with your mother over your stepfather. After all, he's an older man—and older men often seem worldly and glamorous to a younger girl. You may feel yourself wanting to flirt with him and be seductive, especially if he is handsome and charming. Your mother might become upset and worried if she senses this undercurrent of feeling in you.

If you can become aware of your feelings at this point, you can avoid friction between you and your mother and an uncomfortable feeling between you and your new stepfather.

Stepfathers are human like anyone else. They have good points and shortcomings. They have faults and weaknesses, just as they have strengths. You'll probably get along fine with your stepfather, especially if you make allowances for his human flaws and give him credit for his good qualities.

YOUR STEPMOTHER

If you are living with your father and he remarries, your stepmother can become a very important person in your life. She will take the place of your real mother in helping your father raise you. That puts her in a difficult position. She wants to win your love and confidence. Yet there may be times, when

118

your father isn't there, that she has to make certain rules and decisions that affect you. Some kids resent this. She isn't your real mother. Where does she get off telling you what to do?

Some kids grow to love their stepmothers a great deal. Others may get along okay with their stepmothers, but stay loyal to their real mothers even if they don't see them much.

When Angelea's parents divorced, her father was given custody of the children. Angelea's mother was a concert violinist who spent much of her time traveling. Her father's job, however, kept him close to home. It was agreed that the father could provide a more stable home environment for the kids.

After a while, Angelea's father married again. Angelea's stepmother raised the kids with the tender care of a real mother. Angelea liked her stepmother, but she never stopped loving her real mother. Because her mother was so busy with her career, Angelea saw her only occasionally. But Angelea stayed loyal to her. And when Angelea got married, she asked her real mother to occupy the place of honor on the front row at the church while her stepmother sat further back with the other relatives. Her stepmother was hurt because she had loved Angelea and raised her as if she were her own daughter.

The old saying, "Blood is thicker than water," sometimes holds true in these situations.

In most cases, children live with their mothers. If their fathers remarry, there is a different relationship with their stepmothers. When a kid visits his father, his father's new wife is not so apt to be the person who disciplines him. She is not raising the kid. He is only a guest in the home. Of course, the stepmother does have certain rules in her house, and she won't be very happy if the kid disobeys or ignores her wishes. If that happens too often, she might become upset about the visits, which will put Dad on the spot. He wants to see his kids. But he is also trying hard to make a success of his second marriage and to keep his new wife happy.

Some kids find it glamorous to visit their dads and stepmothers. Some stepmoms can be a lot of fun. There is a holiday spirit when the kid goes to visit. The kid is entertained. Dad and stepmom take him to fun places. He doesn't have to study or do household chores. Everybody has a great time.

Then he must come down to earth and go back home to his real mother. The kid may find life with Mom dull and drab. He might wish she were more fun like his dad's wife.

One girl enjoyed visiting her dad and his new wife so much she wanted to go live with them all the time. They tried it that way for a while, but the girl found the situation changed when she actually moved in with her dad. It was no longer a fun visit. It turned into a routine family life. Her stepmother had to set up rules and restrictions just as her real mom had done.

Sometimes, if Dad remarries, you and his new wife will not get along very well. You may be jealous of her. She may want your dad to give her all his attention. Too, she may resent the child-support payments he has to make. You are a living symbol of that expense—alimony and/or child support your father pays to your mother every month. And you are a constant reminder to your dad's new wife that he had loved and married your mother first.

Of course it is to your advantage to try your best to get along with your stepmother and have her like you. That makes it easier to visit your father. And, you have a family bonus that some of your friends may not have. If your parents remarry and you get along okay with your stepmother and stepfather, you'll have four parents instead of two. You'll have more adult support and security around you. You'll have more of a variety of adult role models to help shape your own personality.

STEPBROTHERS AND STEPSISTERS

If the parent you are living with marries again, you may suddenly find yourself in a large family.

A girl named Mary Ann and her younger sister and brother lived with her mother. Her mother's second husband had custody of his four children. Suddenly there were seven kids in the house!

Not all second marriages result in a population explosion like that, but some do. Your new stepfather may not have custody of his children, but they may come to visit from time to time.

Most kids get along fine with their stepbrothers and stepsisters. You have some important things in common with them. You are sharing parents with them. And they have been through the sad experience of divorcing parents, too. So you can be sympathetic.

One problem you may have is the changed age order in your family.

Many experts in human behavior believe that your birth order can have an important effect on your personality.

For example, according to this theory, if you are the oldest brother in your family, you may be used to taking charge of younger children. You learned at an early age to accept responsibility. When you become an adult, you most likely will make a good father, though somewhat strong and dictatorial. You are used to making decisions for others younger than you are.

If you suddenly find yourself living in a family with a stepbrother who is also the oldest brother, you may get along fine with him in some areas and not so fine in others. For one thing, the two of you understand each other. You are both used to being "big brother" to younger kids. But you are not used to taking orders from other kids. If one of you tries to boss the other around, there may be a conflict.

The same thing applies if you are both oldest sisters.

If you were the youngest member of your family and find yourself with stepbrothers who are younger, you will become a middle child. This can have an effect on your life and the way you feel about other members of your family. A middle child doesn't have the privileges and freedom of an older brother or sister. The older children get to drive cars and have dates before the middle child is old enough to do things like that. On the other hand, a middle child doesn't receive the babying and coddling of the youngest. So, a middle child may feel there is nothing special about him or her. They have no special place in the family. Everyone likes to feel a little special.

Perhaps you were an only child. Your parent remarries, and now you have stepbrothers and stepsisters. Only children are used to being the center of attention. They are not accustomed to sharing their parents or their home with other kids in the family.

The matter of birth order and its effect on you can be complex. But it may help you to think about it. If you are having trouble getting along with your parents or your stepbrothers or stepsisters, you might ask yourself if this change in the birth order in your family is giving you problems.

You may have some problems with jealousy. You may secretly resent the time and attention your mother now gives your stepbrother or stepsister. It may take a while for you to begin to like your new brother or sister. It might take some time to become comfortable with your stepparent. But if you can work through those problems, you can have a lot of great new things going for you.

It can be nice, being part of a larger family. Nobody ever suffered from having more people close to them in a family circle, people who care about them. You'll have more people with whom to share your life. And you will be able to share their interests, hobbies, successes, and problems. You can help them and they can help you. Who can knock a set-up like that?

Places You Can Go To For Advice And Help

These days, most communities have organizations that can help children who are having trouble at home or personal problems. There is no reason you should feel embarrassed or reluctant to go to these groups for help. They are there just to help kids like yourself.

Many of these groups are operated by the state or local government. Some are privately funded. Some operate through the United Fund or United Way. Some are national and even international in scope and have national addresses and phone numbers. But many are local. The names they are called may be different from one town to the next. So, if we gave you a specific name such as "Crisis Intervention Center," you might not find that exact name in your phone book. However, that does not mean you do not have a similar group. It may be called something else in your town. If you can't find what you are looking for in your telephone directory, you can ask your school counselor or teacher. If they don't know, phone your newspaper, local library, police department, city hall, city health department, or county sheriff's department. Your church secretary or minister is another good person to go to for this information.

The organizations that have national headquarters usually have the same name wherever they are located.

We'll talk about the kinds of problems kids like yourself may have, and where you can go for help. If the organization has a national headquarters, their address and phone number will be given.

After her parents' divorce, Linda felt a special kind of loneliness. She was an only child and lived with her father. She wished she had an older sister or friend that she could talk with about growing-up problems. Then she found she could have a big sister through an organization called "Big Sister." Through this group, she made friends with an adult who was just like a big sister. They went places together and talked about things Linda wanted to know. It helped Linda a lot to have an adult of her own sex with whom she could relate.

Boys, too, can find a "big brother" this way through the Big Brother group. National address: Big Brothers of America, 220 Suburban Station Bldg., Philadelphia, Pennsylvania 19103. Telephone (215) 567-2748. Big Sisters, Inc., has the same address and telephone number.

Jim had many personal and family problems because his parents were alcoholics. He felt so miserable at times he didn't know what to do. Then he found out about Alateen, a branch of Alcoholics Anonymous. Alateen gives a lot of help to children who have an alcoholic parent. Here, kids meet other young people their age who have to deal with the problems they face. They share their troubles and learn how to make their life better. You can find your local chapter by

124

looking under Alcoholics Anonymous in your phone book. National headquarters: Alanon Family Group Headquarters, One Park Avenue, New York, N.Y. 10016. Telephone (212) 475-6110.

Becky was so unhappy at home with her parents fighting and getting divorced that she ran away. After a while, she found herself homesick and frightened. She was in a strange city without money. Fortunately, help was as near as the next telephone booth, twenty-four hours a day. And it didn't cost anything to phone. National Runaway Switchboard is a toll-free hotline for runaway teens who need help or want to contact relatives. Telephone 1-(800) 621-4000. Another 24-hour toll-free message and referral service for runaway children is The National Runaway Hotline. Telephone number 1-(800) 392-3352.

Mildred was afraid her baby brother was going to be seriously hurt or killed. Her mother was very cruel to the little child, especially when she had been drinking. She beat and tormented the little boy. There are a number of places a kid can go if he knows about a child being abused. He or she can call a free national Child Abuse Hotline, available 24 hours a day. The toll-free number is 1-(800) 252-5400. Locally, you could contact the police or your sheriff's department or your church. Your city may have a mental health organization that would be helpful. Parents who realize they need help so they will stop abusing their children can get help from a group called Parents Anonymous, 2810 Artesia Boulevard, Suite F, Redondo Beach, California 90278. Your city probably has a local chapter. Some parents abuse their children physically. Other forms of child abuse can be emotional cruelty or neglect, or neglecting to take care of the child's health needs.

If you are afraid you have VD, or venereal disease, you can get confidential information from your city or county health department. Also, there is a national hotline that gives information and referral about VD. It is called "Operation Venus." The toll-free number to call is 1-(800) 227-8922.

Allan wanted a place to go to get his mind off his troubles at home. He joined the Boys Club in his town. This organization provides youth guidance and recreational activities for boys ages 6 through 18. There are organized team sports such as baseball, basketball, soccer, football, swimming, etc., plus social activities. Their national headquarters is Boys Club Federation of America, 771 1st Avenue, New York, N.Y. 10017. Telephone (212) 557-7755.

The Girls Club of America has the same services for girls as the Boys Club has for boys. Their national headquarters are at 205 Lexington Avenue, New York, N.Y. 10016. Phone (212) 689-3700.

Parents Without Partners is a group of single parents who meet regularly, share problems, and discuss how to give children a good home environment. The group also has social activities. National Headquarters, Parents Without Partners, Inc., 7910 Woodmont Avenue, Suite 1000, Washington, D.C. 20014.

Here are some other kinds of services that are available in most communities. The names of these groups may be somewhat different in your city. But if you know they exist, you probably can find a similar organization near you.

Drug Abuse Council. This organization provides family and individual counseling for parents whose children use drugs. Psychological testing and counseling for users.

Family Counseling Service. Services include individual, family, and group counseling on personal or family problems. Parenting training and instruction in parent-child relationships. Minors can be seen once without parental consent.

Family Outreach. Counseling for families in troubled situations involving their children. The aim is to prevent child abuse and neglect.

Mental Health-Mental Retardation. Services include psychological testing and evaluation and psychiatric interviews for parents and children.

Crisis Intervention Center. A 24-hour counseling service by trained volunteers for anyone who needs help in a crisis situation.

Your local hospital emergency room. Twenty-four hour medical emergency service.

Suicide Prevention. A 24-hour service by trained volunteers for persons who are severely depressed.

City-County Public Health and Welfare Department. Provides such services as pregnancy testing, maternity care, birth control education and counseling. Medical checkups for well children, and other health advice and testing.

Church-sponsored services. Various denominations in your city probably offer youth and family counseling, recreational programs, weekend retreats, summer camps, and other services.

Battered Wives and Children Shelter. Many cities now have a place where mothers and children can go for help if they have been beaten by the husband.

Many of the groups listed above offer services that are free. Some have a sliding scale charge based on the amount of money you or your family earns and can afford to pay.

How do you know if you need to look for help from one of these organizations? If life has gotten you down so you feel depressed all the time, can't keep your mind on your school work, feel sad and lonely, don't feel like doing anything or talking to anybody, you may need help. If you're confused about your life, can't make friends, or have no place to go after school, the answer to your problem can be found with one of the organizations we have mentioned. Perhaps one of your parents beats up on the other, or on you. Maybe you are thinking about running away from home. You might be afraid you have VD or think you might be pregnant.

Maybe you have a lot of questions about growing up, about sex, about life in general and you wish you could talk these things over with an adult you liked and trusted. It could be you have gotten involved with drugs or alcohol. Or you have a parent who is using drugs or drinking too much. You might want to talk to someone about God and your faith and your religion. Maybe you need help in deciding between "right" and "wrong."

These are all questions and problems kids your age face. That is why so many helpful organizations have been created. Learning about them and finding where to go for your particular problems is one of the smartest choices you can make.

Additional Reading

Encyclopedia of Associations, Detroit: Gale Research Company. Updated periodically. Available in most public libraries.

Galper, Miriam. *Co-Parenting*. Philadelphia: Running Press, 1978.

Gardner, Richard A., M.D. *The Boys and Girls Book About Divorce*. New York: Jason Aronson, 1971, paperback, Bantam.

Richards, Arlene and Wills, Irene. *How to Get It Together When Your Parents Are Coming Apart*. New York: David McKay, 1976, paperback, Bantam.

Roman, Mel and Haddad, William. *The Disposable Parent*. New York: Holt, Rinehart and Winston, 1978.

Woolley, Persia. *The Custody Handbook*. New York: Summit Books, 1979.

Index

About The Author

Charles Boeckman is a prolific writer. Over 1,000 of his stories and articles have been published as well as 27 books. Many of his published articles have been on topics of psychology, health, and family relations. His suspense short story "Mr. Banjo" was selected for anthology in *Best Detective Stories of the Year, 1976*. Many of his books are for young people, among them *And The Beat Goes On,* a history of popular music and *Cool, Hot and Blue,* a history of jazz. His books have been reprinted in Sweden, France, England, Spain, and Japan. Mr. Boeckman, a native of Texas, was born in San Antonio and has traveled all over the United States and Mexico. He now lives in Corpus Christi with his wife and daughter.